SFBT AND THE SOLUTION FOCUSED UNIVERSE:

Creative Applications from SFU Members

Table of Contents

G. Solution Focused Work in School Settings

H. Solution Focused Work with Marginalized Populations

Postscript: Story Telling and Solution Focused Therapy

About This Book

Anne Rambo

Solution focused brief therapy is an evidence-based model of brief therapy in widespread use worldwide. Yet it has been criticized at times for leading to a "cookbook" approach to therapy, lacking in creativity, and for a lack of diversity (Kim, 2013). In 2016, Elliott Connie founded the Solution Focused Universe (then called the Solution Focused University) to reflect a different approach to teaching and training the model. Since then, the Solution Focused Universe (SFU) has grown exponentially, to over 300 members. This book tells the story of the inception of the SFU, and the team that directs it, and then presents snapshots of different SFU members describing their diverse and creative approaches to their work. Differing areas of work, are highlighted, and after the discussion of each area readers will find reflection questions to help reinvent and energize their own work in the field. The SFU hosts a free online community, The SFU Free Public Facebook Community, and readers are encouraged to join this group and continue their creative explorations. Through community and inclusion, we find creative energy for transformation.

Reference:

Kim, J. (Ed.) (2013). Solution-Focused Brief Therapy: A Multicultural approach. San Francisco: Sage Press.

Part One: How the SFU Came to Be

Elliott Connie, *Founder and President*

Adam Froerer, *Director of Research and Training*

Anna Francis, *CEO*

Cecil Walker, *Trainer*

From Founder/President Elliott Connie

My love affair with the Solution Focused approach started just as any magical relationship would—with passion and blinded by love. However, just as with many relationships, pain would eventually break my heart. This book is a step in the healing journey for me, as I regain the courage and strength to move forward. The contributors to this book come from what has become the leading training community in the Solution Focused field, but for me it's more than that; it's my professional home! This book showcases the amazing and brilliant minds that reside within this home. My wish for this book is for you, the reader, to understand why this community and its members are so special. To do that I have to take you back to the beginning of my love affair with Solution Focused Brief Therapy (SFBT) and share a bit about the heart break, but bear with me, it's also an epic redemption story.

How It Started

The very first time I heard about SFBT was about half way through my graduate studies. At this time I had focused on other approaches, but nothing fit for me. I was frustrated and, if I am being honest, was beginning to wonder if this field was for me. Then it happened; I heard about a way of working that was all about hope and helping people become the very best version of themselves. It truly was love at first sight. To this very day, I can't explain it any better, it was love at first sight. As the professor explained this approach that evening in class, I could feel a passion igniting in me. It is a passion that still burns within me now. I wanted to learn everything about it. I wanted to master it. I wanted to be the very best clinician I could be. I had finally found the approach that would allow me to accomplish that aim. I was in love.

The first years were amazing. They were filled with wonderment and discovery as I uncovered new aspects of this approach and myself. I loved every minute of working with clients within this way of talking, and I loved sharing what I was learning with colleagues. As I stated earlier, in those early days I was blinded by love and couldn't anticipate the hardships that were to come. The first adversity I faced occurred within my first field placement during the internship portion of my master's studies. I was seeing clients at a mental health clinic that wanted all of their clinicians and interns to use Cognitive Behavioral Therapy (CBT). I was upfront from the beginning about the type of therapy I was doing and they hired me anyway. I foolishly took that as I sign that they were okay with me using the solution focused approach in my work; I quickly realized I was wrong.

I won't go into detail about all of the things that happened during my time at that first agency, but I will share that the leadership at that organization considered me a threat and worked to get me to stop doing solution focused work. The reason they viewed me as a threat was both a surprise and a lesson for me. This agency had a ten million dollar contract to provide CBT services to youth in a drug court program. When I was added to that team they allowed me to do SFBT with my clients. However, when my clients began to improve at a faster rate than the clients of the other clinician, things began to change. I was originally excited about this. From my perspective, the quicker clients improved the more clients could be served. On one fateful day I learned the harsh lesson that not everyone shared my excitement.

On this particular day I was called into my boss' office where I saw her boss and his boss. I had just walked into a meeting with three people who were far more senior than me to discuss my work—I was terrified. However, that fear quickly turned to anger when they explained to me that I would not be allowed to do SFBT going forward. They explained that too many of them were getting better too quickly. According to my boss and her bosses, people were noticing my clients getting better and had started asking questions. The kind of questions that were a threat to the agency's contract. I was furious that they would put finances above a person's life. I resigned my position the next day.

The Heart Break

After that experience I eventually went into private practice so that I could practice therapy as I saw fit. The freedom was amazing and I flourished, so did my business. Almost immediately I was flooded with clients and felt my solution focused skills growing. Then I did something crazy, I wrote a book. I had never envisioned myself taking on this kind of a project. I had never seen myself as an author. However, as I developed my own thoughts and ideas about SFBT I wanted to share what I was learning—my first book was born. Once again I was excited and blinded by love. Through the process of writing this book I realized there was a global community of others who used this approach. I was super excited to attend my first event of others that also loved this way of working.

I will never forget attending that first event; I felt as if I had found *my* people. I had found a community that felt like home. We all had similar education levels, we all did similar work, and most importantly, we all loved SFBT. However, there was one difference between me and every other member of this community, I was black. In those early days I didn't realize the impact my race would have on my acceptance within this community. I was blinded again because all I wanted was to fit in.

As I experienced oppression and outright racism my heart broke—in fact, it shattered. I questioned everything about my work and using SFBT. This book is not about the details of the racism I experienced, it would take a thousand pages for me to tell that story, so instead I am going to try to talk about the impact the racism had on me. Rejection is hard for anyone, but when you are rejected for things you can not control, things like race, gender, etc., it is especially painful. I was feeling that kind of pain! For those first few years I refused to let myself believe it was racially driven, until the evidence was too strong to ignore. As it was previously, it would be too much for me to go into all of the details here, but what I can say is many of the established professionals and organizations took racially driven actions to oppress me and my career. I tried to ignore the rumors, I tired to ignore the hearsay, but I couldn't ignore the hard evidence. The emails people forwarded me and the recorded conversations made it very clear. It was tough and I had to accept the reality. I spent many days turmoiled and many nights crying myself to sleep. The community I once thought would be home had become my place of torment. I was crushed and heartbroken.

The Redemption

As painful as those experiences were, they had a profoundly positive impact on my life and my work. In fact, I would go as far as to say that the people that tried to destroy me accidentally ensured my success and helped me find a love that I had never known. Having no professional home for my work, I didn't know here to turn. With the support and love from people like Adam Froerer, Chris Iveson, Evan George, Harvey Ratner, and Bill O'Hanlon, I created a community that would stand for love and acceptance. This organization would stand for these things while training clinicians the solution focused approach. The Solution Focused Universe (SFU) was born.

The SFU community not only became my professional home, it became my place of healing. I love this community. The Solution Focused Universe has grown to become the global leader in Solution Focused training. A fact I'm incredibly proud of. However, what makes me even more proud is that this community is based on love and acceptance! No one else will ever have to endure the hurts and pain I suffered. This is a book about that kind of healing! It's a book about that kind of love. Every page and every word promotes that kind of love and healing. I was given the honor of writing the opening chapter of this book and I hope I did that honor justice! I hope you enjoy finding the love and acceptance in the remaining pages of this book. Enjoy.

From Adam Froerer
Adam Froerer is the research director for the Solution Focused Universe

My journey with SFBT has been intimately connected with research right from the beginning. When I was a doctoral student at Texas Tech University I attended the SFBTA annual conference for the first time in 2006. It was at this conference that I heard Janet Bavelas and her colleagues talk about the work they were doing with microanalysis. Looking at the minute details of communication and how language could be used to create change was immediately interesting to me. After this conference, I spent many hours working with the microanalysis team on various projects and completed my dissertation looking at how SFBT therapists use formulations in their work. The microanalysis work taught me that understanding what was happening IN the sessions was as important as understanding what happened BECAUSE of the sessions. This is where my passion for process research was born.

I later served for several years on the SFBTA Research Committee and worked to get SFBT recognized as an evidenced-based approach with various registries. This long, confusing, and often tedious work, was vital to keep SFBT relevant in an era of empirical support and positive outcomes. It was during this process that I grew to understand that an evidence-based status was as much a political status as it was an empirical status. Getting SFBT recognized by the Office of Juvenile Justice and Delinquency Delinquency Prevention (OJJDP) as a *Promising Practice* and by the Substance Abuse and Mental Health Services

Administration (SAMHSA) as an *Evidenced-Based Practice* was challenging and controversial. There were some in the SFBT field who thought this action went against the "non-manualized and non-prescriptive" approach that was consistent with SFBT. However, I and the others on the research committee felt that securing an evidence-based status would ensure that insurance companies would be willing to pay for SFBT services, that agencies would be willing to adopt SFBT as a viable option, and that individual clinicians could have confidence that they were using an approach that had positive outcomes. This work helped me appreciate (more fully) the value of outcome research.

My research efforts continue with an emphasis on making the research applicable and available to SFBT researchers and clinicians alike. I would love to decrease the knowledge-gap between empirical researchers and clinical practitioners within the SFBT field. In this effort I, with the help of others, have recently spearheaded making the empirical SFBT research more accessible. Our SFU research group has begun the process of consolidating all SFBT empirical research (quantitative and qualitative as well as process and outcome) available into one location. This resulting database, *Search Solution Focused Brief Therapy,* can be found at https:// research.solutionfocusedbrieftherapy.com/searchable-database/. This database is valuable because it can be updated continually and makes research, not only findable, but connects researchers with clinicians who are using their work. I hope this database will ensure knowledge flows back and forth between researchers and clinicians much more freely.

Despite having a growing knowledge and appreciation for the SFBT research, my real interest lies in ensuring that clinicians, and thereby clients, get the care and help they need. One of the reasons I was willing to leave academia and my job as a university professor (after 11 years) to work with Elliott Connie and Anna Francis at the SFU, was that I could see how the SFU approached teaching and training very differently from other organizations. The SFU places real value on showing actual work with clients and explaining in great detail how the conversations are being co-constructed and what is happening within the clinician's head during these conversations. This teaching method puts the process research I have focused on for so long into action. I feel that fully understanding this process makes clinicians better at their craft, and therefore, more flexible in their approach when working with their clients.

From the beginning of my relationship with Elliott, I have been eternally grateful that Elliott has been so free with sharing his work. Shortly after we met each other, Elliott shared a recording of a session he had done with a couple. I was impressed with Elliott's generosity and bravery with this seemingly simple act! Not many people have ever been willing to be this vulnerable, before that, or since that time. Little did Elliott know, but I would pull apart each and every word of the session trying to understand how Elliott had already become so good at his craft. I became even more grateful for Elliott's vulnerability when I called Elliott with literally three full pages of questions from the first session. While I peppered Elliott with question after question, Elliott's most common response was, "I don't know". Elliott didn't know why he asked certain questions, he didn't know why he chose the specific words he had used, and Elliott didn't know why his pacing was so quick. Basically I was astounded that Elliott could be SO good and not know the answers to these important questions. I insisted that Elliott HAD to know and that others needed to know why Elliott was doing what he was doing, because it would make the SF field better. I was immediately convinced that Elliott was the key to understanding HOW this approach worked. Elliott was the best I had ever seen do SFBT. Elliott's humble response, time and time again to my insistence that he had to know was, "I'll go find out."

For years Elliott and I have worked in this way. Week after week, Elliott would share his brilliant work and I would analyze every single second and every single word. We would likely both agree that these resulting conversations were some of the most valuable conversations we have had. This willingness to cherish each other's thoughts, opinions, strengths, and abilities was the foundation of something wonderful. Most importantly we learned that our differences, both in opinions and in work qualities, were actually our greatest combined asset!

The overt differences between us were questioned several times in the subsequent decade. After watching Elliott face overt and covert racism in the SFBT field, I realized that I would need to take an overt stand in support of Elliott. After being told to "be careful who you associate with" and after being rejected to collaborate on a project together by the SFBTA, I resigned from all work that didn't include Elliott. I was determined to work with the best, and that meant working with Elliott. I redoubled my efforts to understand what Elliott was doing and to help others understand how they could try to be as good as Elliott. Once when someone was accusing me of discriminating because of my singular focus on Elliott's work, I responded with, "Elliott is the most generous in sharing his work. Elliott is the most willing to reconsider how he is doing his work and doesn't get defensive. Elliott is the clinician who is the most consistent in his approach. And, Elliott is the very best. I choose to focus on the very best so that I can replicate the very best. When you are willing to show me someone better than Elliott at SFBT, please do! I will happily look at that work too." Needless to say, I haven't heard from that individual since.

I find my partnership with Elliott invaluable! Beyond our working relationship Elliott and I have become brothers outside of the therapy/research arena. I have invited Elliott to his home many times and my children consider Elliott an uncle (an uncle who spoils them). My wife puts up with our antics because she knows that I am happier when Elliott is around. We both have, not so secretly, declared that it is this aspect of our relationship that is actually the most meaningful. Working together is great, but being family is really the most important thing. It is because of this relationship that we have been able to demonstrate how SFBT clinicians should view each and every person they encounter. When society was telling me I and Elliott shouldn't be friends because of their different background and cultures, and when the SFBT field was telling us we shouldn't work together because of our different approaches and skills, I and Elliott both knew that none of that mattered because we truly valued each other and understood that it was precisely because of our differences that we should value one another. We know that life is richer when we appreciate the variety the world has to offer.

I love doing SFBT research, but I value connecting with people even more. I love knowing why and how SFBT works, but I value teaching people that they must view each individual they encounter (inside and outside of the therapy room) as competent, capable, and awe-inspiring even more. I loves working for the SFU, but I value the relationships I have because of this work even more.

From Anna Francis

Anna is a Registered Counselor in New Zealand with an online private practice, working primarily with survivors of sexual harm, and is the co-owner and CEO of The SFU.

Unbeknown to me, I started preparing to be a Solution Focused Brief Therapist in early 2005 – on the birthdate of my youngest son, the same day he suffered a profound brain injury. It was on this day and all the days following that I had to dig deeper than I knew was humanly possible. A newborn on life support, two preschoolers at home missing their Mum, a young stepdaughter full of excitement to meet her baby brother and a life or death decision in my hands that would, either way, change life as I knew it, forever.

My baby survived and I kept the promise I whispered to him before his life support was turned off. 'If you can hold on and live, I will do everything in my power to make your life good'. He's now almost 18 years old, still loves it when I whisper to him and has been my greatest teacher.

Also unbeknown to me, I spent all these years very busy learning that people are strong, even when they are experiencing feelings of intense weakness. They are resourceful, even when they can't see any realistic way back up. They are hopeful even when the future feels utterly impossible. And they can survive on ridiculously small amounts of sleep!

I learned that even monumental challenges and difficulties are sprinkled with happiness, relief, comfort and hope. Some sprinkles are so small and are harder to see than others but they are there if you're willing to look hard enough, and we owe it to every single client to be willing to look, relentlessly.

"Relentless" is a very common word that you will hear from parents in similar situations to me who also have a profoundly disabled child. The Oxford Dictionary definition is 'unceasingly intense'. The lack of sleep has been relentless, the chronic illnesses and medical issues have been relentless, the suffering, pain and surgical recoveries have been relentless and the silent heartbreak, sadness and fear is relentless. But also the power of seeing my son smile is relentless, the laughter I hear is relentless, and the snuggles and smooches I get are relentless. The strength I see in other families is relentless. Luckily for me the sprinkles amongst the challenges have become easy to see and all the more clear for working from a Solution Focused Approach.

These challenges have given me a focus on how we as practitioners need to view our clients and what we need to do as professionals to ensure we work as hard as we can to stay out of our clients' way so they can see and discover their own sprinkles...especially in the most challenging of situations.

I feel that choosing to work from a Solution Focused approach is a good opportunity to deliberately use all of my life challenges and allow them to serve a larger purpose. I am very sure I am not special. My situation itself isn't a common one but I acknowledge that everyone has their story. Everyone has struggled and been challenged to a degree that had them dig deep, some for longer periods than others, some digging to deeper depths than others, but a dig nonetheless. And every single one of us, as Solution

Focused practitioners, is in a truly privileged position to meet our clients often during their most challenging digs and witness their sprinkles.

When reflecting on what I do in my work that helps me stay on track and not get caught up in my own head, I remember that despite the problems my clients are experiencing they have continually survived. I remember that each client has successfully survived every single challenge, and how they did that varies greatly for each person. It may not have always served them in the best ways but they still somehow manage to keep going. This is evidenced by simply showing up to their session which for some is a huge challenge in itself. So remaining relentless in my pursuit of bringing to light all the sprinkles they relied on, to move in the direction they want to go, is my only option.

Below is a story of one of my clients whom I would describe as 'book worthy' level inspiring.

Sarah (not the client's real name) comes from a culture where leaving her abusive husband brought shame to her family. She was a well-educated woman but entered into an arranged marriage and moved to the other side of the world to New Zealand alone, barely even knowing her new husband or the new culture she was to be living in. She was very isolated and living with abuse not only from her husband but also members of his immediate family. She had managed to escape after several years of extraordinary suffering and at the time of meeting this remarkable woman she was seeking support due to severe depression and anxiety. We met on 3 occasions over 4 months. These were not smooth sessions for either of us. These sessions had me questioning the approach given just how huge her struggles seemed to me, and how out of my depth I felt, but each session she turned up and she answered all of my questions and I chose to stay the Solution Focused course. Our time finished with her describing and experiencing some small successes of happiness despite the overwhelming weight of her struggles to build her confidence, seek employment and obtain New Zealand residency.

Six months after the 3rd and final session I received an email from this client wanting to inform me of 'all the good things happening' and how our sessions had been useful. She shared several successes stating that in the last several years she was at her happiest and wanted to share her 'proudest moments'.

There were many amazing takeaways for me after meeting this woman so early on in my Solution Focused career and I have reflected on them many times since. These are my takeaways:

- We don't always get to see our client's progress and successes, so it's important to trust the process, trust the research, trust the client and work hard to trust ourselves.

- No matter how huge the client's problems are, they are still capable of change. I learned to not allow my own frame of reference to inform me in any way.

- When we question the modality we're really questioning our confidence in using the modality. Looking back on the times I questioned the modality it was due to my struggle to find a 'good' next question. It was due to my feeling overwhelmed when my client was having a visibly hard time. It was due to allowing my lack of belief in myself to creep into the session.

- I learned that I needed to keep practicing. Learning this approach is like learning a language so the more I practiced the more my doubts about both the modality and my ability to use this approach well, started to fade away.
- I learned that "I don't know" isn't a scary answer to my questions. Our client may be moving into uncharted personal terrain and may be about to discover something amazing about themselves they hadn't yet been aware of.
- I learned that amazing things can be discovered in the awkward uncomfortable silence and learned with time that that turns into a comfortable space for the sprinkles to brightly shine.
- I learned that my relentlessness allowed my client to rediscover hers.

These takeaways have stayed forever present in my work which has allowed me to continually grow as both a counselor and as a facilitator and trainer within The SFU. It has also ensured that burnout hasn't come knocking. I love all of the roles I play within the SFU, but above all else I love doing the actual work, sitting with clients and having conversations about change and possibilities. I am fueled by my clients and I am confident that each and every conversation is a gift of inspiration I doubt I would see or feel in quite the same way, had I chosen a different way of working.

I knew as I entered my counseling studies that I wanted to use one way of working and do it really well, rather than using many ways of working and doing them all just 'ok'. I didn't yet know what modality would catch my attention but as soon as I learned about Solution Focused Brief Therapy I instantly knew this was it. This was the only way I wanted to work with clients, the only way to view my clients and this was how I also hoped all of the professionals I had ever had dealings with during my son's life viewed me. I have tried to live my life by my mother's mantra of 'treat others how you'd like to be treated' and I think that Solution Focused Brief Therapy is the perfect modality to allow me to do exactly that.

I can't help but imagine how different the world would be, how differently all humans would truly feel about themselves if the only way we could view and treat one another was through the lens of relentless resilience, capability and resourcefulness. The global change in humanity would be monumental with just that small shift. My magic wand doesn't hold that level of power but it certainly warms my heart that I can do that for my clients, that they can feel truly seen for all of their brilliance even when they don't yet clearly see it themselves. It's a start and the more of us doing this work the larger the ripple effect will be.'

This can be a challenging mindset to master given that we're socially conditioned to seek help for our mental health by taking our issues and problems to a professional to talk through and unpack. I remember finding it really hard to navigate through the 'problem talk' when I was finding my feet within this approach and often found myself wanting to help 'fix' things or offer words of encouragement – I now recognize this was, in part, my wanting to remove the discomfort I was feeling in the session.

What helped me move through this was my love of reading true stories of survival. 'True and tragic' is how I describe the genre. From a very young age and even now, these are the only kinds of books I enjoy reading. My first memories of such a book was the courageous story of a woman who led a group of Jewish children from Poland to Israel at the time of the Second World War, titled 'My Hundred Children'. I also read the story of Helen Keller who was an amazing woman who lost her sight and hearing after becoming ill at 19 months old. My most recent read '3096 Days' was a story of a young woman who was kidnapped as a child and held captive for 8.5 years before finally escaping. These stories of extraordinary resilience have helped me to develop a Solution Focused mindset.

'I had never thought about why I only liked reading 'true and tragic' stories. I also really love watching the crime channel on tv so assumed I had a bit of a twisted morbid curiosity but as I started to do this work more I realized that after being with clients who shared their stories of survival, I had the same overwhelming sense of inspiration and a million questions about how could they have gone through all of what they had endured and still be sane or even alive! I also began to realize that I didn't need to hear my client's stories to be inspired by them, I learned that everyone has their story. Simply showing up began to be enough to view them as resilient, capable and resourceful people and I knew they were survivors of their life no matter what had caused them to come to therapy.

The details of their story in a 'problem talk' way started to matter less and less and seeing them hear their own answers to my questions mattered more and more.

Questions like: 'How did you cope through such a difficult time?' and 'What strength did you draw upon the most?' and 'Sitting here now after sharing your experience with me, what would you say you are most proud of with how you coped through that?'. If I could be so wowed by someone who's story had been published in a book I could then also be wowed by any client who sat before me. Following this realization I noticed I got stuck a lot less often and my next question became easier to find. I noticed I was doing a lot less thinking about what to ask and a lot more listening, looking for the sprinkles to color my questions with. I could dig deeper in my search with more ease rather than skimming across the top and catching what was already visible. As my confidence and skills evolved my work began to create more meaning to the client and I saw change quicker and more visibly.

I feel certain that my confidence, skills and 'obsessive love' of this approach could not have blossomed in the way it has without coming across The SFU and its incredible community of fellow Solution Focused practitioners. It provides me with a safe and nurturing place to learn and grow. I feel extremely privileged to now contribute to the learning and growing of others.

From Cecil Walker
Trainer, Solution Focused Universe

One of the greatest benefits to a career as a mental health clinician is the enjoyment of contributing to something more meaningful than your own personal needs and individual perspective. That benefit is also one of the distinctive features of the Solution Focused Universe. Every person who participates in SFU trainings, events, gathering, and social spaces gets to experience a very noticeable sensation of working towards something significant and good. Everyone carries an unspoken certainty that something very important is living in the heart of these conversations, these questions, and these interactions, and that something important could help change lives for the better. It seems to be rare that an organization can run on the hope for change for the better, but it's even rarer that it's accompanied by an assumption that everyone can change and is worth the effort. The SFU is a place like that, and its greatest currency is intangible but noticeably felt by everyone who comes in contact with it.

I first came in contact with the SFU through Adam Froerer. He was my professor in graduate school. At the beginning of the first semester of my MFT program, Adam announced that he always had ongoing research projects and was happy to have the help of any students interested in joining him on those projects. At the time, I had just finished my undergraduate studies where I worked in a psychology research lab. I enjoyed my work in research and knew I could use the extra stimulation to keep me busy now that I suddenly no longer had the hectic schedule of an undergraduate student, so I emailed him asking how I could help. Adam proposed that I join him in a microanalysis studying presuppositions that he and a clinician named Paula Lange were about to start. As just a graduate student, that microanalysis study showed me all the very intricate intentions that go into successful solution focused sessions. We very literally examined every word uttered by expert clinicians during a recorded session with clients covering the work of SFBT greats from Steve de Shazer to Elliott Connie. I learned how to construct a solution focused conversation sentence by sentence.

As we moved through the study, many interesting findings and noteworthy points of interest were standing out to us, so we thought it would be fruitful to discuss those points in a presentation at the first SFU conference in Niagara-on-the-Lake, Canada when the opportunity arose. It was at this conference that I got to experience the fullness of the passion and the skillful mastery that propels the SFU's work. I had learned so much about the details and the technique of the solution focused approach from studying the transcripts inour microanalysis, but attending that first SFU conference felt like a masterclass in all the other necessary but hidden components, the compassion, It was at this conference that I got to experience the fullness of the passion and the skillful mastery that propels the SFU's work. I had learned so much about the details and the technique of the solution focused approach from studying the transcripts in the energy, the intuition, the attentiveness, the imagination, the relentless belief in an individual, etc. I felt like I was making strides in figuring out more and more about how to master this approach with new realizations and progress every hour of the conference. Conversations with and teachings from the brilliant minds of Chris Iveson, Peter Tzabo, Wendel Ray, and Rayya Ghul were all fuel for a lot of mental calculus as I was piecing together how to make sense of the philosophies and skills attached to solution focused work. The greatest good I got from this first experience with the SFU was an introduction to a remarkable way of looking at people in general.

The only way to use the solution focused approach well is to view individuals as competent and deserving. They are experts in their lives, in their relationships, and in their desires. They're also deserving of opportunities to change, to learn, and to grow. It's probably accurate that many people would agree with these sentiments in general, but I don't think everyone is constantly carrying that assumption at the forefront of their awareness as they move through all their interactions with others. It makes a difference when you speak to someone in a way that makes this perspective overtly apparent to them, and I left the conference wanting that to inform both the lifetime of clinical work ahead of me as well as how I treat other human beings in general.

For years, I continued to work with Adam on research projects and articles even after completing my graduate program. Eventually, I found myself on the SFU staff joining Adam and Elliott in their trainings and events. Of course the gifts of solution focused work have had an impact on me, but, as I mentioned, the greatest award is the effect I can observe in clients. I went into private practice immediately after graduating and used those first few years as much needed time to sharpen my skills and deepen my fluency in this approach. My office in Midtown Atlanta was a few blocks away from Georgia Tech, so I saw many college students as well as adolescents and their families. There's a lot to be said about the agency and freedom this approach allows adolescents and individuals launching into young adulthood, things they are not used to easily attaining, but the most profound impact of my use of SFBT came when I started applying this approach to an even more uniquely displaced population.

After a few years of working in private practice, an urge to give my time and effort to the less privileged had grown to be hard to ignore. It was never lost on me that neither my younger self nor any of my family members would have been able to afford the same therapy I was offering. I gave a sliding scale fee to those who needed it and tried my best to be as flexible as possible, but private practice is a difficult setting to accommodate those most in need. That led me to working for an international nonprofit organization with a clinic on the outskirts of the city of Atlanta. The organization was established to combat the negative effects of torture and human rights abuses. The clients are all refugees and asylum seekers who have experienced some form of immense trauma or persecution. Not only are they carrying very burdensome trauma, but they're also new to the United States and are usually struggling to establish a stable and happy life with few resources and knowledge of their new surroundings. I continued my private practice work alongside this new work and was constantly amazed by what I saw in these clients.

There's been a remarkable range of diversity in the background of the clients that I have seen through this work. When I first started, I saw mostly Central American asylum seekers who left their home countries like Guatemala or El Salvador and traveled by car and foot up to the southern border of the U.S. to ask to enter and plead their case for asylum. Most of them did not speak English and were persecuted by either their corrupt government, local violent gangs, or the dominant majority identity group. These people had been threatened and attacked. Many had been abducted or had their homes broken into. They witnessed loved ones and community members being harmed or even killed. Sometimes their aggressors collaborated with each other to persecute these individuals. For example, governments might allow or even encourage gangs to threaten and attack protesters or political dissenters. The clients who endured this mostly had little or no family in the U.S. and were only coming to escape the risk of further persecution. They were all under the reasonable assumption that either they successfully make it to the U.S. or they can expect to be eventually harmed. As difficult as those circumstances might be, there's a new layer of problems that arises once they do make it to this country.

Most people aren't entirely familiar with the differences between an asylum seeker and a refugee if they're even familiar with the experiences of refugees at all. Refugees are internationally recognized as having been displaced by some political disaster such as civil war, government corruption, military/police targeting, etc. Many of the world's more stable and industrialized nations work together to provide resources, safety, and opportunity for these displaced peoples including allowing a certain number of refugees to enter and become legal, permanent residents of their countries. There are multiple steps to the process of becoming a legal refugee and being placed in a new country, but each step of the way, an individual is under the care of some organization, nation, or authority charged with ensuring that they are given what they need to survive and pursue a new, safer life. Even once they've moved into their host country, the government and/or local organizations are responsible for supplying them with resources and opportunities to rebuild a sustainable life for themselves and any accompanying family. In the U.S., refugees are given health insurance and have access to government assistance for food and shelter. They often have access to free English classes and other programs aimed at helping them adapt. All of this demonstrates that, in the grand scale of the underprivileged, refugees are at least accounted for. Life is difficult for them for numerous reasons, but they at least have the constant assurance that some institution or governing body is responsible for them and their needs as they get back on their feet. To be an asylum seeker, however, is to have all of the same difficulties without any assurances of help, accountability, or responsibility.

The main difference between asylum seekers and refugees is that asylum seekers flee their threatening circumstances on their own and personally ask for entry at the border of the U.S. without the help or processing of a refugee organization. That means they are not guaranteed access to a permanent new life in this new country. It is internationally accepted that any human being has the right to request asylum from danger. Any country that recognizes internationally accepted human rights has to accept these requests for asylum. While the United States does affirm these rights by allowing asylum seekers entry, it could very well be argued that the processes that this country puts these individuals through still verges on threatening to them and their rights. Anyone who enters at the border requesting asylum is automatically detained; they are essentially imprisoned until they are processed and able to pay exorbitant bail fees. Once they are released from detention, which can sometimes take several months, they are entirely on their own and responsible for taking care of their own needs despite the fact that they are legally not allowed to work for several more months until they receive a work permit. Any help or resources they receive are entirely voluntarily through nonprofit organizations, religious institutions, or the generosity of individuals. They have virtually no access to healthcare or educational opportunities unless they can somehow afford out-of-pocket payments. They are not even seen as legal residents as refugees are. They are seen by the law as temporary visitors who eventually need to prove they have good reason to be here permanently. On top of the trauma of the experiences that drove them from their home countries, they essentially live in a foreign place not as someone seeking refuge from harm but as a suspected criminal assumed guilty of entering into the U.S. under false pretenses unless they can competently prove otherwise through a long and arduous legal process that can take several years before providing them with a trial that determines if they are permitted to stay permanently or if they will immediately be expelled back to the country they came from.

Life for both refugees and asylum seekers is extremely hard. It's even more disheartening when you consider that these individuals also expected that they would be safe from hardship and many of their worries once they could be within the borders of the U.S.; they traveled here with the hope that if they could make it, everything would be easier, but it rarely works out that way. This immense hardship makes it all the more impressive to see the many moments I've witnessed of undeniable progress and hopeful ambition. Of all the people on Earth, this population has some of the most indisputable reasons to expect the future to hold more fear and dissatisfaction, but that is not how they respond in therapy. The most common reaction I get from others hearing of my work with refugees and asylum seekers is that of fear and worry; most people expect that work with this population is tiresome, burdensome, and an immense sacrifice to endure. But every single session I have with these clients is quite the opposite. Instead of the vicarious harm that is often assumed to accompany this very trauma-centered work, I am constantly filled with a vicarious renewal of hope and trust in human tenacity. Instead of feeling like their woes and trauma have splashed onto me, I constantly feel reassured that individuals can withstand big, difficult things and keep moving.

Through my solution focused work with these clients, I've been lucky to personally witness people with some of the most severe physiological and psychological symptoms recover and reform into a version of themselves that is happier and more hopeful and at peace. I've seen a woman, after fleeing with her partner from their home country because of the violent harassment they endured for their same-sex relationship, describe the relief she experienced in being able to hold her partner's hand at the grocery store and not feel afraid. I've seen a young student activist, who was brave enough to protest against her government and who faced abduction and literal torture as punishment, restart her life; she feared and distrusted every person she came into contact but eventually lost a bit of that fear day by day until she found herself working, dating, and living a fuller life, things she assumed she could never do. I've seen a man who lived through war, a civilian cursed to constantly witness neighbors and family members bombed and killed and who later suffered from severe memory issues as a result of his intense PTSD. He told me repeatedly that he can't remember details from day to day like what he ate, who he talked to, or how he spent his time, and he certainly can't remember things from far in his past. Within our solution-focused conversations, he was able to recall his childhood, being raised by his now deceased mother and all the hopes and dreams she had for him that he passed onto his children. It feels like such a gift for me to sit across from them all as they transform into someone they thought either was lost or was never possible to be. Part of what is so remarkable about moving through this process with them is that there is really no way for me to personally prescribe to them how to fix their problems or heal the wounds of their experiences. The most powerful moments are when they teach themselves about what moves them just a little bit further and what eases their pains just a little bit.

I saw a woman for almost a year who was chased out of her home country by a gang with the intention to end her life and harm her loved ones. When I met her, she told me she had nightmares most nights and could not keep herself from replaying all the many terrible things that happened to her to people she knew. Even if she could get her thoughts under control, her body was stuck in a state of heightened fear and exhausting vigilance; she could never feel at ease. It's at that point, once I've know what they've been through and what ailments they're currently suffering from, that it's the easiest for me to be afraid or doubtful that I can be of any help for such big problems. But as always, I kept moving forward in our conversation, intent on finding the other half to her story, the part full of drive and motivation to do hard things. Before all the events that rerouted her life, she worked for years as a school teacher to small children. She felt like that was her greatest purpose on Earth. In fact, raising her own son is what pushed her to continue to deal with threats and harassment and then eventually to try to find asylum in the U.S. Now in a new country and her son fully grown, she felt disconnected from any sense of purpose and felt all she did all day long was be hurt and afraid. But as we kept talking, she mentioned that she did notice a lot of her symptoms lighten when she recently got to visit some family that also lived here in the U.S. She got to play and laugh with her cousin's young daughter and was now recalling in conversation with me that she didn't have any nightmares that night and that the next day she had forgotten to be scared for large parts of the day. Over our next few conversations, she recalled more and more moments that revealed to her how possible it was to feel alright in this new segment of her life, even after all the things that had happened to her. When I would ask her where she got the strength to do such difficult things and move forward through so much uncertainty, she would remember she'd actually always been pretty strong. When I'd ask, how does she continue to call on the strength she needs, she says she'll whisper it to herself and read a bit out of her bible whenever things feel a little rocky. One of the moments that was most impactful to her in our conversations was when she realized that after having gone through all the things she faced, including nearly dying, and then moving to a new country without the language, skills, resources, or relationships necessary, all of that was so unimaginably hard and scary that nothing else could possibly happen to her now that could outdo that. She's already faced the most difficult thing that could happen, and she conquered that difficult thing. In telling me all these beautiful things about herself, she was reformatting how she sees herself and the relationship she has with the life she is living. But she's not the only one who gained much needed reminders; she and all the other clients constantly remind me how any person could find their way to a little more peace, a little more happiness, and maybe a little more certainty if you ask just the right questions and notice just the right things.

Part Two: Creative applications by members of the Solution Focused Universe

In Medical Settings

In Coaching and Consultation

In Conflict Mediation

In Addictions Treatment

In Community Based Mental Health

In Private Practice

In Schools

With Marginalized Populations

Special in memoriam section: Storytelling and SFBT

Author Biographies in order of contributions:

1. Deb Bush is a registered nurse psychotherapist in Canada working part-time for an outpatient mental health clinic; she also has a part-time private practice and she is a founding member of the Solution Focused Universe.

2. Adam Lake is a GP (primary care physician) living and working in Lancashire, UK. He works as a doctor in NHS general medical practice and teaches at Lancaster Medical School. He enjoys family life with his wife and three daughters, leaving the occasional spare moment in which he watches Blackpool FC, runs in the countryside and plays guitar in a blues band. He is a member of the Solution Focused Universe.

3. Erica Jo Ramos is an Occupational Therapist, Psychotherapist in Toronto, Ontario, Canada. She has a mental health OT private practice and is a member of the Solution Focused Universe.

4. Paut Struik runs her own business as a Solution Focused consultant, facilitator, trainer and coach in The Netherlands and is a founding member of the Solution Focused Universe.

5. Vinay Nair runs a private psychotherapy practice, Happy Minds Café, for client therapy and coaching. He is a corporate IT sales leader and a passionate trainer in the SFBT modality. Vinay is a long-standing member of the Solution Focused Universe.

6. Angela Hayes is a licensed marriage and family therapist and master life coach in Round Rock, Texas and a founding member of the Solution Focused Universe.

7. Niki Lee Rowe is a certified mediator and New York State Licensed Mental Health Therapist. For over 30 years, Niki has learned to trust in mediation as the pathway to beneficial outcomes for those experiencing conflict. In 2016

Niki began to experience the value of applying a solution focused approach to the meditation process. Niki is Certified with the National Board of Certified Counselors. She hold a certification in Anger Management Therapy, and has with her solution focused team developed a Solution focused Anger Management Program. In 2008 she and her business partner published a national manual on '*Investigations in Long Term Care Facilities*'.

8. Marcos Perez LaMadrid teaches at the Universidad Mayor de San Andrés (UMSA), and coordinates a program which strengthens family protection services in rural areas of Bolivia. He is a founding member of the Solution Focused Universe.

9. Melanie Bray is a Registered Social Worker/ Psychotherapist in Ontario, Canada. She has been working in the field of mental health and addictions for the past 20 years. She is a founding member of the Solution Focused Universe.

10. Rachelle Bloksberg is a licensed therapist in private practice in California, who specializes in tele-therapy from a solution focused perspective. She is a founding member of the Solution Focused Universe.

11. Donna Harper-Hinton is a Canadian Certified Counsellor, Certified Solution Focused Therapist, and a member of the Solution Focused Universe. She was an International Educator and School Counsellor and is now in private practice.

11. Chris McMullan is a social worker and a school-based therapist in Woodburn, Oregon. Chris works with elementary children in the district offering solution focused brief therapy as well as engaging in public speaking events about "Finding our Hope". He has developed expertise in supporting children and has found his true purpose in the work he is blessed to do each week. Chris is a member of the Solution Focused Universe.

12. Rebekka Ouer is an openly queer licensed clinical social worker, author, and owner of her private practice in Dallas, Texas, where she has passionately specialized in solution focused work with the LGBTQ community since 2011. She is a founding member of the Solution Focused Universe.

13. Anne Rambo is a professor of family therapy, who works with her graduate interns in the school system in Fort Lauderdale, Florida. She is a founding member of the Solution Focused Universe.

14. Edward Eisemann was a much-loved figure in the solution focused community, and a founding member of the Solution Focused Universe. He worked in New York City for years with homeless and street youth. He was known for his wonderful metaphorical stories, three of which he contributed to this book.

SOLUTION FOCUSED WORK IN MEDICAL SETTINGS

Deb Bush *(registered nurse psychotherapist)*

Adam Lake *(primary medicine)*

Erica Jo Ramos *(occupational therapy)*

Deb Bush

My journey towards solution focused work began with my nursing degree from an Ontario university. I was trained in problem-based learning and embraced the learning modality that taught students how to learn, rather than what to learn. My final placement was in a mental health unit, and I was hired there immediately after graduation. However, I quickly found myself in an environment that did not mesh with my inner compass.

I felt determined to find something that worked better. I had struggled myself through university and helped a family member through significant mental health challenges, so I saw people having these experiences as just that, people having experiences, rather than as a diagnostic label. I was drawn to Dr. William Glasser's work. In 2009, I obtained a certificate in Reality Therapy using Choice Theory. While the ideas appealed to me, I found the model simply wasn't sustainable in a traditional psychiatric environment, with little support.

I decided to leave the healthcare setting and try another mental health environment that would better suit my orientation. I moved from the emergency department, to a public health position where I could work more directly with clients and the environment in which they lived - seeking to empower mental wellness and prevent deterioration in mental health in younger generations. I accepted a job with Public Health in the public school system, kindergarten through Grade 12, counseling, linking individuals to the community, and building on the individuals mental health skills. My focus expanded from looking at symptoms I was assessing, to a wider focus on context, so that I was collaborating with students, parents, teachers and administrators and encouraging perspective shifts through collaborative conversations using Collaborative & Proactive Solutions by Dr Ross Greene. With changes in Public Health, my position that supported bridging the frontline with system approaches was no longer supported financially and I was forced to a crossroads of remaining in Public Health or moving back to the healthcare system.

I decided to move to the healthcare system in an outpatient setting and was introduced to solution focused brief therapy. I was energized by the information learned and went on to earn a certificate in the model from an Ontario university. I credit Elliott Connie's work and the Solution Focused Universe with truly helping me hone my craft. Solution focused work gave me the mindset and confidence I had been looking for to enlist the client's best hopes, notice their own resources, explore their history and future desired outcomes and to embrace the clients themselves as allies in the process.

Armed with my solution focused understanding and skills, I started my own private practice and I have been advocating at my current place of employment, which requires a cognitive behavioral approach (CBT). The provincial government and healthcare system recognizes CBT as the evidence-based approach for psychotherapy. They see therapy as teaching, where I have learned over the years from my varied experiences, the power of language, conversation and people's innate skills. I coped with the different perspectives using my passion, perseverance and humor and what I call "stealth" SFBT – incorporating a solution-focus into the required discussions. I have been called on the carpet more than once for my approach, however many of the clients I work with improve! Despite some colleagues who criticize the approach, some have referred clients to me – because they have noticed the clients I work with get better, and "somehow" the work I do works. Below are just a couple of examples of the power of such solution focused conversations.

Case 1:

I worked with this client for three sessions using solution focused brief therapy. The client was diagnosed with Major Depressive Disorder with Psychosis. At the initial meeting, the client presented with thoughts described as paranoia, fear of returning to work worried about what colleagues would think of her and concern about the "bridges I burned". When asked what she hoped for, she wanted to have her joyful, easy going, free spirit back, her smile and sense of humor. The client hoped that the difference this would make was "increased confidence, meaning, and peace with her faith".

Throughout the time of the three sessions, she began to have an interest in reading again and reading books she found inspiring. While she was on a walk, she felt a feeling of faith return. She noticed that she had an ability to have heart to heart conversations with those she cares about again. She had family for dinner, her father noticed her ability to relax as they set the table, she noticed herself observing others taking the lead and reflected on how she let them. She spoke of the many intentional efforts she and her partner made to create an engaging, inviting, and welcoming environment and of her ability to have conversations and be at peace. She noticed her "clear mind" which allowed her to focus on what was important to her. She began visualizing meetings with clients, which was for her a sign that she was ready to return to work. This was a new experience that she had not had in a while trying to return to work over the past year.

She returned to work and reported that things went well, she was welcomed back despite how she left. She noticed a difference in her ability to work since this experience. One colleague shared that they noticed a difference in her, a "freeness" in her interactions with others. She noticed her ability to have tough conversations and came away with the thought "they are entitled to their opinion and I too am entitled to my opinion", instead of losing sleep over the interaction. She noticed and identified many changes - a balance with her care for others and her objectivity; her ability to work with colleagues more effectively; her understanding that she does not have the pressure to fix anyone but rather hearing and supporting them in some of their most difficult times.

She was able to share with her supervisor her readiness to take on new challenges, to bring calmness and the "real her" to each new situation. She found the feedback from clients and colleagues inspiring and she described her appreciation of such. She was able to identify supporting people and identified their strength through difficulties she shared. Her partner's jokes with her about work she saw as a sign of their ability to support each other through this transition. "Good things are happening" she stated at the last session. She felt her confidence and the freedom she was hoping that she could regain.

Case 2:

I worked with this client for five sessions. The client was diagnosed with Major Depressive Disorder (MDD). It was clear that dwelling on his current circumstance, going around and around with his thoughts, his loss of perspective and his feeling slow and struggling with his memory led him to sadness and feeling depressed. What he was hoping to work toward was a more objective view of himself, more awareness, an ability to think and to express himself clearly, to share his perspective and opinions at work and to be present at home rather than being lost in worry. The difference he hoped this would make was to feel purpose and passion again and to have improved relationships with his family.

He articulated progress through the sessions. He noticed himself focusing on what he had learned over the years, the transferable skills he had developed and what he was passionate about rather than focusing on resentment about how he was being treated at work. He created a plan to share with his boss and on an interest he had for a project that was not yet assigned to anyone. He noticed his ability to focus on creating the action plan and goals for the rest of the year. He noticed himself leaning into his faith and reaching out to friends that he had not spoken to in a long time. One friend texted him back "glad you are feeling better". He spoke about his drive and actions of reaching out to colleagues for feedback. Since he was not getting clear direction from his employer, he created some direction for himself. He started applying for new work opportunities. He was crying less and he was able to delegate tasks more. He was submitting things on time at work which was a change. He started using a notebook to assist him with his memory challenges. He noticed that he was surrounding himself with people who inspired and supported him.

He applied for a position and the interview went well. He noticed confidence during the interview as he reflected on his past. He was thoughtful with his applications. He specifically looked for opportunities that validated his skills, had opportunities to work from home, and that were in desirable locations. When he was preparing his resume and preparing for the interview, he noticed his ability to lean on friends for support as he took on this new challenge. He reflected that he would take deep breaths and have thoughts of "I can do this" despite the stress. He noticed feelings of happiness, being capable and feeling accomplished. The interview had given him confidence to keep applying no matter the result. "I am capable," he shared. Despite challenging environments at his work place he continued to make an effort to share his opinions despite being dismissed. He noticed himself thinking "I am doing the best I can".

He got the job he interviewed for and accepted it. He got all the work completed to set up his old workplace well. He closed the loop with other colleagues in other locations. He noticed thoughts of resolve as he strived for his next step. He was thoughtful about advocacy to support his current team as much as possible. He acknowledged the proud feelings he was experiencing. These decisions at work influenced him to reconnect with his family in meaningful ways.

Case 3:

I worked with this client for four sessions. The client had been off work with a diagnosis of Major Depressive

Disorder (MDD) and Generalized Anxiety Disorder (GAD) after a brain injury a year earlier. The client used to drive big machinery and he wanted to return to work, which the doctors were telling him he was not ready for. As he spoke of his past and all that he had accomplished, his confidence grew. At his second appointment, he shared that he had looked into colleges to study something he would be able to do. The person he spoke to about options ended up giving him an interview as a college professor. The college advisor saw through their conversation experience and listing his skills that would support this role. At the third session he shared that he got the job. He shared details of the differences people around him noticed including his doctor, who gave him back his license.

Adam Lake

I have long felt that the medical model is too narrow an approach to deal with the whole range of human difficulties which primary care physicians often find themselves asked to help. Where social, emotional and psychological difficulties are concerned it tends to locate difficulties inside the minds and brains of individual people with its talk of chemical imbalances and neurotransmitters. However evidence for its theories and approaches, especially psychopharmacological ones, is lacking and evidence of harms mounting, necessitating for me a wider search for ways to interact with people when they entrust me with their hopes for a better future - a huge privilege and responsibility and I want to do them justice.

My search led me to earn a diploma in psychotherapy, then to a detailed review of the evidence for psychiatric medications and their potential harms so that I could fully inform patients of the latest research, then later through BRIEF and the SFU, fully immersing myself in the stance and practical language practice of the solution focused approach. It was only then that I fully realized how radically different and effective this approach is and I then came to almost exclusively flip between the medical model and the solution focused approach. This was a gradual and organic shift, as of all the approaches I learned in my diploma studies and had attempted to integrate I was finding asking solution focused questions to be the most effective and efficient way of talking with people in a setting where I have 10 minutes each with 30-40 patients. The approach also seemed highly acceptable to most patients and was associated with an increase in beneficial outcomes. As Mark McKergow says, this approach takes the focus out of people's brains and heads and more appropriately to the 'in between', the infinitely complex interactions between people and their environment. I have found a 'home' here in an approach which complements the medical approach very well, shines the light of attention on and amplifies the beneficial change that is constantly occurring and fully respects people's autonomy and expertise in their lives.

The first significant learning point has been the effect taking a solution focused stance can have - leaving some space for deliberately setting aside diagnoses and labels and looking at the person as a human being who is motivated for something to be different, is doing the best they can, and has successes and resources to draw on can create openings and possibilities. In some ways, rather than being an objective assessment, the act of asking questions determines to an extent the picture that emerges. It can be a difficult balancing act, and I have to ensure I am getting all the information I need to do my job safely - but keeping this stance in mind can make a difference. Case examples follow.

Case Example One:

Consider 'a twelve year old boy with behavioral difficulties who is verbally aggressive, impulsive and hyperactive affecting school and home' and whose best hopes are 'to be calm and get on well with people', who excels at playing football and despite frequently feeling angry, more often than not chooses to take himself off to his room and manages to calm down by himself as he 'doesn't want to upset his family'. Same person, depends what questions are asked and where attention is focused. In one of Jacqui von Cziffra-Berg's training courses I heard her describe a metaphor which I have found useful: imagine a small dot on a blank page - information necessary to do my job is still gathered and acted on appropriately but rather than focus on the tiny fraction of his life experience on which attention is directed if purely 'diagnostic' questions are asked, he may see himself a little differently if attention is also directed to all the space around this, and surely this is a more ethical way to work as well.

Case Example Two:

The second way in which training in solution focus has helped is being more precise with use of language. I will elicit a patient's best hopes early on in the consultation to give direction to the consultation and also to provide a reference point to come back to if the conversation is unhelpfully getting stuck in too much detail about the problem - 'and if your boss started talking to you like that again tomorrow, but somehow that energy and calm you hope for was present in your life in a way that was just right for you what might you notice about the way you respond that perhaps was a little bit different?". Later, even as I am making an assessment and listening to the person describe the problem, I am also listening out for resources. These might be activities that they enjoy, past successes or, in the case of chronic severe mental health problems, the resources they have drawn on to get through. Indeed the longer and more severe the difficulty the more resources people must be drawing on, and even a question or two exploring these can make a difference. In the midst of describing the problem people very often say things like 'Tuesday wasn't so bad but every day since then has been absolutely awful....'. This jumps out at me and I find myself asking a few details about what they did differently on Tuesday, how they did it and the difference it made. This can sometimes allow subtle shifts to be made, and can also reveal reference points to come back to later on ('suppose that slightly lighter feeling you had last Tuesday began to show up a little bit more, how could you know').

So often, especially in consultations about mental health difficulties, the focus is on the absence of a symptom rather than the presence of what they would hope to see instead, and a preferred future description is another way in which I apply the approach. With the pressures of general practice, it is a huge challenge to consult and write up notes in ten minute appointments at the best of times - but I often now feel compelled to find opportunities in the patient's language to ask a few questions about details of the presence of their best hopes in their day to day lives. This is often only a minute or two and I am careful that such questioning is appropriate to the consultation but people tend to receive the questions gladly and engage with them and informally the outcomes seem to be better than before I started this practice. I will often, as an opening, use whatever we have agreed as a plan and come back to the language given to me by the patient from the best hopes question and throughout the consultation. To illustrate, I recently saw a mum who had recently given birth to her third child and after discussion had decided she wanted some beta blockers for feelings of anxiety she was experiencing that were troubling her. I asked her 'So let's imagine that these medications work exactly in the right way for you and exactly the right way for your life, what might you notice that would let you know?' Her answers and follow up questions led to her saying things like 'I'd be calmer, I'd have more energy.' 'I'd want to get up in the morning' 'About 7.30 probably' 'I'd have breakfast. Toast and jam.' 'I'd be smiling more'. 'Yes, they would be pleased' 'I'd be more present for them' . 'I'd actually be doing things with them'. 'Taking them to the park'. 'They'd actually come to me if they were upset, they've been going to my mum instead of me.' 'Oh, it would make a massive difference, I'd feel like I was really being their mum'. I find that when I hear these kinds of answers I feel a genuine sense of admiration and warmth towards the person which is likely to be picked up by them, and also that I more often have a positive sense of anticipation when seeing them on the list, resulting in a virtuous cycle.

Case Example Three:

Another example was a woman who had previously been given a diagnosis of depression who was having a tough time. We had agreed a plan of some time off work. I switched to the solution focused approach and asked 'if two weeks off from work turned out to be just the respite you needed, and the following week you had all the fighting spirit you could hope for and life was freshened up in just the right way what might be different about the way you woke up on the Sunday before your return to work?, What might be the very first thing you notice?'. There is not typically time to go through a day of course and in this example I asked one or two questions about what her husband and children might notice and how her colleagues at work could know that this fighting spirit was present and 'freshening up' had occurred, and she came back having gone back to work early, had a conversation with her boss about things she wasn't happy with and been moved to a new shop which she was pleased with. If I remember correctly her words were 'I think I realized nobody's going to be able to sort things out for me, I have to be proactive, and I've realized I can do it'. Who knows whether she would have had the same outcome anyway but it seems there's a good chance our conversation helped, and this shift to increase sense of personal agency and autonomy seems to be a common one which is beneficial primarily to the patient but also to the GP and health service as well. It is also interesting that, as in this example, there is so often no relationship really between the presenting problem and the described outcome.

Case Example Four:

People often wonder whether an approach which involves conversation and questions can be helpful in what would be termed 'severe long-term mental health problems'. I have found that it often is in my own experience.

For example, in mid-2020, in the midst of the pandemic, I had a series of six ten minute phone conversations with a lady in her 50's who had had a diagnosis of schizophrenia for thirty years and was ringing in crisis, hearing voices for all her waking hours, very anxious, and sitting on bench by the road when she called. After I had made the necessary assessment including risk and ensured appropriate referrals were made I switched to a solution focused approach and our few minutes of conversation ranged from times when the voices were even a bit less prominent, what was most helpful to her about sitting on a bench outside and the difference it made, and her best hopes for her day to day experience if phoning up to seek help turned out to be just the right thing for her (waking up with things to get up for and wanting to get out of bed). There was time for a quick confidence scale, during which she talked about having previously completely given up alcohol herself without any help from services. Over the next few months our few minutes of solution focused conversation turned to how she was waking up wanting to get up, taking her disabled sister out shopping, had a sense of purpose again. The voices receded to the background and she was enjoying drawing pictures of dogs again and painting. I love working in this way because all the credit for change rightly rests with the patient and there is no way of knowing whether our conversations helped in her recovery. There were no medication changes made and she was yet to see the mental health team, and in fact was much improved when she did see them three months later. Now over a year later there have been some ups and downs but on the whole she is doing well.

These sorts of conversations do often seem to be associated with a higher likelihood of patients making changes which please them, across the whole range of mental health difficulties in my experience. Another case early on in the pandemic involved a 15-year old girl who was cutting her arms several times a week, and through a series of five ten-minute consultations over four months which included detailed descriptions of exception times where she managed to do something different when she felt the urge to cut herself, her skills and interest in football refereeing and hopes of combining sports science course in college, ways she coped when feeling anxious at school, all embedded in the small details of her current day to day life, she completely stopped self-harming and a year on is thriving in college.

Reflections

I make a great deal of use of scaling questions, as they seem to me very effective when time is short as they provide a very useful concise framework from which we can pivot to finding out what is already working and has worked in the past, by asking why their chosen number and not lower, and to some further preferred future details by asking what they might notice if they found themselves half a point or one point higher. I often find they have the effect of increasing hope and sense of competency as well as being an opportunity for them to hear themselves say what is working already.

I will flip between the medical approach and the solution focused approach, but how to decide when each is appropriate? I clearly need to make sure I'm making all the assessments and interventions I need to as a general practitioner (GP), and I have found over the years that rather than mixing two approaches, to then put aside the medical model for period of the consultation works best. One morning I read a quote in a newspaper which really helped clarify this for me: 'Move the authority to where the information is' – having since looked it up it was a quote from a man called David Marquet, a US Navy Captain whose work I am not familiar with, but the idea seems relevant to the integration of a solution focused approach into medical practice. The doctor is the authority on medical knowledge and skills which is of course why people make appointments, and the patient is the authority in the intricate details of their own lives and the ways in which their short visit to see the doctor might alter those details for the better. The authority moves in a fluid way depending on the clinical situation and the point in the consultation - clearly in emergency situations medical intervention is the clear priority, and other times the authority would best be placed with the patient. As an example of a situation in the middle of the sliding scale, when discussing lifestyle I will share relevant information and explain what lifestyle changes are associated with improvement for their condition. Then, rather than advising (as how could we know what changes would fit for them), I will often ask whether they'd be pleased if they moved towards that sort of change, then follow up with some solution focused questions about what they or significant others would notice. This often results in a whole range of responses - things like walking for a paper instead of driving (person with osteoarthritis who wanted to lose weight), a patient's son being pleased his dad might live to see his future grandchildren (man who smokes forty cigarettes a day with chronic obstructive pulmonary disease), specific things like choosing to not put chocolate biscuits in the shopping (woman with poorly controlled diabetes), being able to have breakfast with the children (somebody feeling low who wanted to cut down alcohol). This may increase motivation and likelihood of change but above all feels a way of talking with people which respects their expertise and therefore authority in their own life.

I am optimistic about the growing number of people in medicine using the solution focused approach, with an increasing number of GPs attending BRIEFs training events in recent years. I have spoken at the WONCA Europe family doctors conference (Berlin 2020) about the integration of solution focused practice into primary care medicine, and in September 2021 I spoke at a national safeguarding conference in the UK to a group of GP's about the solution focused approach in medical practice, and alongside a colleague talking about the signs of safety approach to safeguarding children which has grown and developed since the 1990's and is increasingly used in the UK.

Applying this approach significantly increases my job satisfaction. I believe there are other benefits to us as clinicians as well, not least the appropriate sharing of responsibility with the patient, especially where the outcome they hope for involves changes beyond the realistic reach of medical practice. It is talking with and viewing people in a way which fully respects them as human beings with their individual stories, hopes and resources and is an addition to my work which increases patient autonomy and choice; and one that also seems to be associated with an increased chance of a beneficial outcome.

Erica Jo Ramos

I first discovered solution focused brief therapy through a webinar Elliott held on finding the client's 'inner superhero'. The approach really resonated with me and I went all into learning about SFBT and incorporating it into my practice. SFBT is not a common approach used in OT practice and learning more about it really improved my skills as a practitioner and opened the doors to many opportunities, including starting an SFBT department at an agency focused on return-to-work that previously only offered CBT.

In my journey, I find in both solution-focused practice and occupational therapy have a common focus on what works, and on the potential of the future rather than on what cannot be recovered from the past. I find that the philosophy of solution-focused therapy aligns with occupational therapy in core beliefs: clients are the experts in their own lives; I elicit strengths and resources rather than solely focusing on deficits and disability; and the conversations between client and practitioner are hope-filled and practical, helping clients identify small changes in their lives.

I found that solution-focused practice was the missing piece to enhance my practice as an OT. Exploring the desired outcome of what clients wanted out of therapy allowed me to go beyond traditional goal setting in OT and gave me the language to truly hear and connect with the heart of what matters to my clients. As a supervisor to OT students and clinicians, I resonated with some of the challenges they often faced when starting out in practice. Well-meaning OTs often came into sessions, eager to help their clients 'problem solve' by implementing different interventions and educating them on coping strategies, but when clients appeared to 'fail' to follow through on the recommendations, things often started to fall apart. I, too, had this experience and felt disheartened as I felt I was pulling out all of my best 'tools' in the toolbox. But rather than thinking about adding solution-focused practice as another "tool" to add, I decided to embrace the principles behind the approach and apply this wholeheartedly to my practice.

I found that adding solution-focused practice to my practice led to the following: clients were more motivated and engaged with the collaborative approach; they noticed small signs of progress and change and/or ways they have been able to better manage and cope with the difficulties in their lives; they often said they felt more hopeful, that they "felt heard" and that they heard questions that they had never thought about before. As a therapist, I felt reenergized by my work as my clients were readily participating in their own analysis of their occupations (meaningful activities in their lives) as they described their life when things are going well, and through this process, clients often came up with ideas strategies and interventions that best worked for them. I also found that removing "homework" or formal recommendations at the end of sessions removed limits and expectations and allowed clients the creative freedom to trial their own interventions in their lives.

I have worked in several sectors but I have primarily worked within the community with clients who were in motor vehicle collisions. As a case example, one client that I worked with (details changed to protect client identity, the client requested to be referred to as "Carpe" in the case example as in Carpe Diem) was in a collision while riding public transportation. Carpe's injuries resulted in physical, cognitive, psycho-emotional and psycho-social challenges which significantly impacted her life and her ability to return to her activities of daily living, her past job, and leisure activities. One of Carpe's major goals was to return to riding the bus independently (and manage her level of fear and anxiety when riding the bus). Using a solution-focused approach, I found that Carpe wanted to bring out her "inner she-ro" (female superhero) and to "be kind" to herself in order for her to manage her day-to-day activities, and this was a common theme for future sessions. Carpe spoke about how the Marvel superhero character, Wonder Woman, inspired her and she used this as her creative way to motivate herself and develop various coping strategies. Over many sessions, I worked with Carpe to gradually work toward taking the bus (e.g. from talking about riding a bus from the comfort of Carpe's home, to walking together to the bus stop, to sitting and chatting at the bus stop, taking a bus together from one stop and then several stops). Eventually, this culminated in her taking the bus independently and meeting me at a café to celebrate over dessert. Throughout this rehabilitation process, Carpe expressed her "inner she-ro" and kindness to herself in many ways and this was most noted through the progress that she made between the therapy sessions. For example, while sitting at a bus stop she read a poem she wrote about her recovery process and how she felt she was starting to see signs of her old self starting to return. She spoke about how she noticed that she was being more kind to herself as she was accepting help with some tasks around the house and she chose to cook a recipe in a different way that was easier for her to physically manage. In another session, she showed me an abstract painting that she created after a session which represented the darkness from the past but with a sunrise starting to overcome the darkness. She expressed kindness to herself as she decided to wear a bright outfit which represented her inner superhero as she stepped onto a bus for the first time in a year.

Carpe was asked for her permission to share her story above and she volunteered to share the following:

My experience with Occupational Therapy

Traditional therapy is salting the wound and then re-salting the wound on repeat. Yes, one must clean the wound first, otherwise infections may set in and what started out as a small cut turns into a life or death full fledged trama. I agree, I get it. Sometimes you have to revisit the past to understand the origin of said wound?

Yet, continuing to re-open and salt the wound is not only painful but it doesn't only hurt the host, it retraumatises and sometimes delays recovery. Healing becomes just a theory.

I was offered solution-based therapy from Erica Ramos. Eager to recover, I had decided to try any new and alternative ways to get better. I had given traditional Occupational Therapy a chance and, as much as I was happy to be helped, I was disappointed. Erica was and still is an amazing individual who brings out the best qualities in a person. Unfortunately, the traditional methods she was taught could only do so much.

She had planted the seeds of ideas and helpful suggestions. It is up to me to keep the seed watered and nourished. Because I had to bear this responsibility, I had something invested in the solution.

My creative juices began to flow, sometimes it came pouring out like Niagara Falls. I now was inspired to go back to creating and then stopping and even improving upon it. When the ideas come from me, I become invested in how I could improve myself and control my reactions to things I cannot change. I didn't feel as if I've failed upon the expectations of others. My anger subsided as I learned I didn't need to follow a timeline. I can go at my own pace. You cannot race against others when you find the right solution for you that you had a hand in creating."

Questions for the Reader:

1. Deb, Adam, and Erica all work to see the individual in front of them, not just the diagnosis. How can you look beyond medical labels in your practice?

2. What helps you stay hopeful with clients, even when other professionals are seeing these same clients as chronic or hopeless?

SOLUTION FOCUSED WORK IN COACHING AND CONSULTING

Paut Struik *(consultant)*

Vinay Nair *(life coach)*

Angela Hayes *(life coach)*

Paut Struik

I was originally trained as a physical therapist but my interest in larger systems issues rapidly led me into health care and social work administration and management. I can identify the exact moment when I was first introduced to solution focused work. At the time, I was a regional manager for a social work organization focused on supporting people with disabilities. The mission was to increase independence, but the medical model often used was not always helping with that goal. A colleague invited me to a lecture, and I went along on the spur of the moment. The speaker was Vivian Hogg who together with John Wheeler had developed the Signs of Well-Being model for the NHS (UK). I remember thinking "This is exactly what we have been looking for!" We had already noticed that the most successful social workers on my team focused on small steps and daily successes, rather than on diagnosing problems. This new model gave us the language to describe such an approach, and a way to promote it. I immediately got training for myself and my team and we embarked on testing and developing applications this approach, like offering people when they first contacted us a longer conversation about how they had coped so far. Within a few months we saw our waiting list shrinking and clients reporting that somehow things were much better since that first phone call.

Not too long after, my strong interest led me to explore the entire solution focused world, and to step out on my own as an independent consultant. Unlike those who stick to one area or specialization, I have never wanted to be tied down. I consult to local governments, to those in education, to health care and welfare workers, and even to manufacturing organizations. I credit my late husband, Jacco, who was an ecologist and often accompanied me to solution focused conferences, for coming up with the perfect way to describe it: "This is a generic model." The application of solution focused ideas can be universal across human and indeed many biological systems.

One application I have come to love more and moren is that of Solution Focused Peer Supervision. In Dutch and German speaking countries peer group supervision is often called "Intervision". They are meetings where participants in a group or team coach each other, as it were, on work-related issues in a structured way.The most used models were always quite problem focused. Over the past 15 years our team at Vraagkracht in The Netherlands have developed many ways of doing Intervision in a Solution Focused way .This has since been welcomed and adopted by hundreds of teams in The Netherlands and Belgium.

We also train and coach people who want to learn more about facilitating Solution Focused Intervision. Intervision can be used in case consultations, by a team that wishes to adopt new practices, in management teams that would like to coach each other and develop their work as a team, to practice and to further Solution Focused skills and as the go-to place to be inspired by like-minded others. Intervision groups ideally consist of five to eight or ten people, but larger groups are also possible with some modifications. Members usually all have the same role or position in one company. In 2014 I introduced the concept of 'Open Intervision' with participants from varying backgrounds and/or jobs or organizations. The Solution Focused approach makes for a very safe environment and the participation of professionals outside one's own circle helps with asking questions from a not-knowing position and generates more out-of-the-box thinking. In appreciative or Solution Focused organizations, the manager or team leader is welcome to be a member of the team Intervision group.

Participants describe the Intervision sessions as fun and to the point. They also report that it deepens their understanding of their work and builds their confidence in their Solution Focused skills. The team building aspect of Intervision contributes to the change they wish to see in their organizations. A bonus is that they all become more familiar with the skills and knowledge of their fellow workers, which adds to team collaboration and success. Another interesting observation is that participants often find answers to their own questions, even if they have not put it to the group to be discussed. They get ideas for their work that they were not actively looking for. Managers and team leaders report that teams that have regular Intervision sessions become more independent and resilient and enjoy their work more.

The intervals between team Intervision sessions can be anything from a week to a month six weeks. The effect seems stronger with a higher frequency. The length of Intervision sessions can vary. If they are held weekly, an hour is often enough. If the interval is longer, two hours is a better choice. On average one question takes about half an hour; less with more experienced teams. At Vraagkracht the team uses a variety of Solution Focused Intervision models.

Below, I describe one model[1] which is always very popular and shows the possibilities of Intervision.

Overall process: One group member at a time gets to put their question or dilemma to the group (the client). This question or dilemma is then discussed– in a structured manner – with the aim of helping their colleague acquire new and useful ideas.

1. The facilitator suggests that the client begins their question with "How can I ..." The facilitator then asks:
   a. What is the main reason behind you asking this question?
   b. Tell us about your dilemma.
   c. Could you describe to us, in five to ten sentences max, the context of your question? Talk about things that might be useful for us to know, so that we can give you suggestions that will be most useful to you.
2. The group then asks questions like:
   - What have you done so far that worked?
   - On a scale of one to ten, one being: I am totally at the beginning and ten is: yes, I can close the case/ the project is finished successfully..., where are you now? What puts you at this number already?
   - Suppose a colleague were to ask you this question or come to you with this dilemma, what advice would you give them?

---

[1] Based on Norman, H. Solution Focused Reflecting Teams in O'Connell, W. & Palmer, S. (Eds). 2003. Handbook of Solution-focused Therapy. Sage Publications. http://www.sagepub.co.uk/book.aspx?pid=103667

- What solutions for your dilemma have you already thought of yourself?
- What have you tried so far that has not worked?
- You clearly have thought about this a lot. What ideas have you come up with already?
- What did you do in earlier situations like this that worked?
- Suppose we don't come up with the right ideas, who else could you ask?

3. The facilitator then asks things like:
    - How have our questions so far been useful?
    - What questions would you have liked us to ask that we didn't?
    - Would you like to rephrase your question at this time?
    - If you would like to rephrase your question, what would it be now?

4. Now the facilitator moves to the Appreciation Round. The facilitator says to the group: "Briefly tell your colleague the one thing that impressed you the most about him or her, based on what you just heard, like: - I admire … - I am impressed by … - I envy how you … It's okay to repeat a compliment if a person before you says exactly what you wanted to say. It just makes the compliment bigger! The colleague (our client) just listens and does not respond, other than maybe to say thank you."

5. The next step is about tips and ideas.
    a. (To the colleague/client) "Just listen and write down what makes you curious and what you might want to remember."

b. (To the rest of the group) "Give your colleague your tip or idea in a concrete and clear way, in one sentence, starting for example with: - I would … - Remember … - You could read … - Go and talk to … "

c. Let the group go several rounds. Ask the colleague/client after a while if he or she has heard things that could be useful. Or you could continue till everyone has run out of suggestions.

6. Reflection by the client could be introduced with: "On a scale of one to ten, where one is: this was a total waste of time and ten is: this was the best decision I could have made today, to ask you guys this question, where on the scale would you say you are right now?" And perhaps you would like to ask something like: "What could we have said that would have made it just a tiny bit higher?" Note: The rest of the group does not ask any more questions or add tips or suggestions at this point.

7. This part of the Intervision session ends with thank you's all around and the group then moves on to the next question.

There is a lot more to be said on the how and why of the different elements in this process, but they all contribute to the Solution Focused principle that it is the client that ultimately decides what their next step will be towards their desired outcome. In addition, questions asked out of genuine interest and that push for minute details all contribute to change in the direction of this outcome.

Summary:

Solution Focused Intervision works well for strengthening teams and professionals. It requires a skilled facilitator with a good grasp of the Solution Focused approach, but the participants do not necessarily need to be trained in the Solution Focused approach. Intervision has proven to be a profound and yet fun way to deal with complex situations, strengthen bonds and promote a uniform approach in a team or an organization. Intervision can be an important resource for any professional to help them deliver their best work and prevent burn-out. Intervision is flexible in its form and application and can be used in a variety of settings. It is my best hope that Intervision can contribute to work satisfaction and peer support. This is something we need even more in the coming decades with a diminishing work force and more people needing care and support from dedicated professionals and leaders.

Vinay Nair

"Change begins with hope and is always a question away".

2018, the year I met Elliott Connie, was a marquee point in my journey in psychotherapy. I had finished my master's in psychology and was at crossroads about the modality to practice counselling. I was never for being eclectic! While I had a full-time job in Information Technology sales (which I still hold) I wanted to make a mark in psychotherapy and coaching/training. The reason was ever evident – to facilitate the process of growth and change in people's lives. I wanted to ultimately see changes in my life. But I wasn't comfortable having problem-talk for hours on end to find solutions and outcomes that people (clients) would eventually seek. That's when my introduction to Elliott and SFBT through his keynote speech in Bangalore, India, happened.

Listening to his speech, SFBT made a lot of sense. Having come out of a long hurtful relationship I had a story of mental fortitude myself. Elliot's keynote only reiterated my belief in creating conversations of resilience. Thus began my SFBT journey, learning its nuances and the difference it could make. While the impact it could make in Sales was a no-brainer, its long-term benefits in preserving and building relationships were palpable. I was only too cognizant of the long-term effects ego and conflicts could have on couples and other relationships. SFBT is the anti-dote that any relationship would do well with.

I have always been fascinated by people and why they are the way they are. SFBT reiterated the importance of being non-judgmental which I already was by virtue of my life experiences. With a lot of years in technology sales, SFT brought in a new dimension to my sales approach. While a problem statement was still relevant, my conversations shifted towards the outcomes my clients sought from the platform I offered. Today, often on calls, one of my favorite questions is "Once the solution is implemented, what other strategic activities would your team focus on? What would you start noticing in your processes that lets you know the software/solution is adding value to your operations?"

Every client is unique. So are the sessions. I've learned over time that SFT is simple yet not easy. I continue to use it in client interactions, be it on sales calls or in therapy sessions. SFBT affords the space to follow the process with a clear view of the client's desired outcome. More importantly, it lets me, as the therapist, shun prejudice and be non-judgmental. A case in point was when a client said, "when I'm myself I would give myself the time to be sad and be critical of myself". With SFT I didn't have to question the intention of the thought but just ask, "what difference would it make to you to give time to be sad and critical of yourself?".

SFBT enables me to chase my professional passion too – being a Trainer/Coach. It's a profession that brings me enormous joy every time I take the stage. India is a land of training/coaching opportunities. SFBT has opened avenues for workshops and training, both corporate and in educational institutions. Very little compares to the joy of facilitating the process of learning.

A very recent workshop I conducted on "The Power of Presuppositions" in an international conference is a classic example of how training impacts the community. In a place like India where SFBT is relatively new and untried, training gives me the opportunity to disseminate the possibilities of optimistic therapeutic intervention that SFBT brings about.

Being an SFBT practitioner has brought me a deeper understanding of the culture I'm in. While psychotherapy is still taboo, clients are open to counseling sessions to pour out their problems. Many times, I've seen therapy used as a safe space to vent life's unfairness and frustrations. Combine it with deep outcome focused conversations and the clients experience a decluttering of the path forward. As a therapist, it's especially gratifying when a client says "Ahh, I didn't think of it that way until you asked me that question". I've noticed that SFBT lends the client a degree of freedom to express themselves without the fear of being judged or misconstrued. Once, a client started by saying "I'm not going to talk about any of my problems, I don't even feel like talking." I responded by saying "That's okay. So, what are your best hopes from our session today?" The client was taken aback – I rephrased the question – "At the end of the session, how would you know that this conversation was helpful and worth your time?" The client said I would get out of my room more often. The conversation continued...

The realization that culturally SF1.0 fits in better in an Indian scenario has been a revelation. Sitting with the problem statement and acknowledging where the client is coming from before asking for the best hopes eases the process. In my private practice, I've had to patiently sit through problem talk, often leaving me befuddled. But it has also enhanced my ability to shut my inner voice, take a "not-knowing" stance, and listen to their curious case of overcoming their tribulations. It has given clients the opportunity to revisit their strengths, resilience, and resources that they seem to have disregarded. This "Indianizing" of SFBT helps build a meaningful conversation in a culture that likes problem solving.

SFBT lets me engross in conversations of opportunities, past successes, and tenacity. In a recent session, a client, a veteran sales leader facing anxiety due to changing company culture, was able to reminisce how he maneuvered through tough market conditions and team dynamics. More importantly, he could connect back with his proven strengths and what his family had noticed about him over the years. Questions like "what do you know about yourself that lets you know that you can sustain the changes and grow?" and "who in your family has noticed these strengths and expressed it to you?" have been pathbreaking.

The discovery of how SFBT brings significant others into the conversation has been enlightening. I once asked a client, "Where did you learn that taking small steps and one day at a time was important and the right thing for you?" The client said "I learnt it from my mom. She had a tough life and taking a day at a time was the only way forward". The value that relationships can add to a person's journey is astonishingly crucial. It's also something that clients often forget when they aren't in the right place. SFBT accentuates the history of the value system instilled in clients and its importance in achieving their desired outcome.

My SFBT journey is on-going, and the lessons are never ending. I've realized that conducting an SFBT session in Indian regional languages is a challenge. That's work in progress. There are times when it's painstaking but the smile on the clients' faces when they discover their way back makes it worth the while. Making that gentle yet assertive move from problem to best hopes and resources available for change to creating a picture of a transformed future is always an exciting proposition. Isn't that what the helping profession is all about?

Angela Hayes

I am a licensed marriage and family therapist and a master certified life coach in Round Rock, Texas. I specialize in working with couples and families as a solution focused clinician. I was blessed to be introduced to solution focused brief therapy early in my MFT master's degree program and experienced a feeling of connection with SFBT right away, while still feeling completely baffled about how to do it. I threw myself into learning about marriage and family therapy and began attending conferences and trainings, in addition to my university studies. The second conference I attended was hosted by AAMFT in Austin, Texas and it had a lot of great topics; however, I was most excited to see one about solution focused brief therapy. It was called *SFBT: A new description* and was being taught by Elliott Connie and Dr. Adam Froerer. Adam and Elliott did an amazing job of teaching the model in a way that made it accessible. Elliott shared a video of one of his sessions and I remember thinking, "This is it! This is what I want to do." That was the day I truly fell in love with the model and I have been practicing and training in SFBT ever since.

One of the beautiful things about SFBT is that it doesn't just apply to therapy because at its core SFBT is a stance; it is a set of assumptions, values, and beliefs about change that influence what we are curious about and how we view and engage with people. It is a way of being with people and a way of communicating that is uplifting rather than "just" a set of therapeutic interventions, which is how it is often perceived. The solution focused stance is being used in education, coaching, police work, medical offices, and so much more. One piece of advice for those who are new to SFBT is to really entrench yourself in the solution focused stance rather than just trying to master the "techniques". Often people who have tried SFBT and say "it didn't work" are attempting to do the interventions within the context of a problem focused session. The techniques are powerful but are most effective when embedded within the context of a session based on solution focused principles. Taking the time to really understand and absorb the stance flows smoothly into doing the interventions in a really authentic way and leads to new interventions that are uniquely your own. As Adam and Elliott have said, learning SFBT is like learning a language. You can learn a set of phrases without understanding the language but once you are fluent in a language you can use it to say anything.

One of the things that I began noticing as I attended trainings and participated in solution focused practice sessions, on both sides of the "couch", was a pattern of solution focused communication that grew among trainees and was modeled by instructors. This pattern of communication was evident in the way the participants noticed strengths in others as they shared about challenges they faced or even complained about something (the famous 'Moan, moan, moan" exercise from Rayya Ghul), and in the transformation these exercises created in trainees. The trainees experienced a shift in what they were curious about, what they noticed and attended to, and how they communicated with one another. I also noticed this transformation as a participant in the communities of solution focused practitioners through the types of questions they ask one another, the kinds of things they write blog posts or do podcasts about, and how they offer support to one another.

I noticed a shift in my thinking, assuming, and communicating that impacted the way I spoke with my spouse and children. It changed my parenting style. It made a huge impact on how I approached asking for what I needed from people which led to deeper and more meaningful relationships. One of the assumptions of SFBT is to pay attention to what works and do more of it and I was paying attention! Another important assumption is that change is always happening.

When talking about SFBT and why I am so passionate about it I often tell the story, with my son's permission, of the moment that this shift in thinking, seeing, and communicating really sparked for me. The story is about an interaction between my son and I when he was a young teen frequently struggling with emotional regulation. One day he had become very dysregulated about something, I was holding him in my arms as he struggled and yelled. It was upsetting and frustrating for both of us and yet I remember noticing as he struggled that although he could have easily hurt me or even break my glasses, he didn't. What a profound realization that even though he seemed out of control he was still careful not to hurt me. I told him, "Bub, I know you are really upset right now but thank you for not hurting me and keeping me safe." and suddenly he just stopped. He stopped struggling and yelling and sat while I hugged him and we began to talk. We were able to have a conversation about what he was feeling. It was a magical moment, a powerful moment that brings tears to my eyes even now, years later. This wasn't therapy, this was just a mom and son and the difference that a solution focused change in thinking, seeing, and communicating made in a difficult moment. As this way of thinking and communicating developed for me, I began to see possibilities for how this could help clients. This was the beginning of my conceptualizing positive communication, which is a style of communication based on solution focused principles.

When I began thinking about positive communication as something that could help couples build stronger relationships, I really struggled with the dilemma of taking on a teaching role while holding a non-expert stance. As a solution focused therapist, it isn't our job to teach and yet sometimes we have to set the role of therapist aside to do other things like assessments, providing resources, and safety planning. We do our best to do those things in a solution focused way, evoking the solution focused stance as a way to do that, but therapy gets set aside at times to do other work with clients. I found direction in the wisdom of Insoo Kim Berg in "More than Miracles: The State of the Art of Solution-Focused Brief Therapy" which recounts a debate between Ms. Berg and another therapist who suggested that solution focused therapists never give advice to which she responded, "What? You mean that if you knew something that would help the client, you wouldn't tell them? (de Shazer, et al., 2012/2007, p. 155). On the other hand, it is important to uphold the client's authority and expertise in their life, to approach teaching as a tentative offering that may add to an already existing foundation rather than from the idea of correcting a deficit and take the time to explore the client's best hopes and look beyond the strategy of better communication.

Solution focused therapists push beyond the strategy of "better communication" to what difference better communication would make in the relationship, exploring when they have communicated at their best and what that looked like, looking for instances of good communication in the present and past, identifying what is different in the relationship when good communication is present, and creating a preferred future description of that difference. This is powerful therapeutic work that can create deep and meaningful change for a couple in a short period of time! The shortest path to a change is always along the path that is already there, even a little bit, which is going in the right direction. This is the heart of solution focused couples therapy and it focuses on accessing and amplifying what the couple already has to help them move forward in their relationship. It is not a teaching role. So, what does that mean as we try to move between these two roles? It is important to be mindful of what mandate you received from the client and what they are requesting to receive from you. If clients are asking for therapy, we do therapy. If they are asking to learn to communicate better, that may be an opportunity to explore what positive communication could add to their relationship. Ultimately one cannot perform the role of solution focused therapist and solution focused teacher simultaneously, they are two different jobs. Think about your experience with attending training for solution focused brief therapy, where you likely experienced a solution focused teacher and discovered you were already doing so many things well and you increased your learning and skills. That is very different from your experience role-playing as the practice client, the stance is the same and yet the two roles, therapist and teacher, are very different.

Anyone who has ever worked with couples knows one of the main strategies they will focus on to improve their relationship is communication. This is not necessarily the best time to put on your teaching hat! It is important, just like with any other solution focused work, to thoroughly explore the client's best hopes before moving forward and explore instances when the best hopes have been present. Couples who might benefit from positive communication find it relatively easy to answer questions about their best hopes, are able to make positive observations about their partner, and demonstrate that they are accurately understanding what their partner is sharing in the session (versus hearing them through a trauma filter, for instance). They typically do not have a lengthy history of being in conflict with one another and will often express an interest in making their relationship even stronger or have noticed not communicating as well after going through difficult times or significant change. They will often leave a "first session" feeling renewed in their relationship and feeling seen and heard by their partner and reiterate their hope of learning better communication at a subsequent session.

For couples who are concretely requesting to work on their communication and who appear to be good candidates, I tentatively offer positive communication skills. This is a departure from the solution focused diamond approach, but one that I find useful. I let couples know that some have found it helpful to explore how they communicate in more detail and notice what works best for them so they can do more of it. Understanding the parts of positive communication is important for us as teachers, and I believe I can also share that information with clients if they might find it helpful or if they ask for specifics. If they already have their own language for these concepts then I always want to defer and use the client's language instead.

Introduction to Positive Communication

Positive communication has four parts: 1) acknowledgement and validation, 2) *and* rather than *but*, 3) making a specific, detailed request rather than a criticism or a complaint, and 4) sharing what difference receiving the request would make for the speaker or why what they shared is important to them. Typically, being more intentional with any part leads to clients reporting positive changes in their communication with one another and an increase in mutual understanding and connection.

Example:

I noticed you got the kitchen cleaned up and I really appreciate it. I can see you worked hard to get all the dishes put away. *[acknowledgement and validation]*

AND, *[and, rather than but]* in the future, I would also like the trash to be taken out if it's mostly full to make it easier for me to start cooking dinner. *[a specific request]*

I feel loved and that my work cooking dinner is valued when the kitchen is ready for me when I get home. *[difference or received value]*

Parts of Positive Communication

Acknowledgment and Validation

One of the things that we strive for in couples' sessions is for both partners to hear affirming things from the other partner. In a therapy session we are going to construct careful questions to elicit those affirmations which can sometimes be really challenging for couples to answer in the beginning. Most couples who are good candidates for positive communication express that they notice their partner's contributions but just didn't mention it or haven't been as attentive as they used to be. They are able to easily answer questions about it and to share their understanding of their partner's perspective and experience.

When working on communication skills, we can bring this to the couple's attention by asking questions about how they feel when their partner notices their contributions and shows understanding of their point of view. What do they notice others doing that help them feel understood and listened to? What difference does it make in the relationship when those acknowledgements are verbally shared rather than just silently noticed? Exploring this often leads them to notice even more and to be intentional about expressing it. It is common when going through challenging times to verbalize frustration and distress and we sometimes forget to be just as verbal about the good things! Starting with an acknowledgement or a validation is like starting a session with "What's been better?". We are focusing on thinking about and noticing what that the other person is already doing, even a little that one values and sharing it with them. For example: "I noticed that you've been more mindful of putting away devices during dinner and it makes me feel closer and more connected to you." It is also an opportunity to acknowledge their perspective, priorities, or challenges they may have. For example: "I know that you have been really busy and stressed with work because of that big project."

People often spend a great deal of time collecting a list of the things that they are unhappy about which generally leads to them feeling more unhappy and unsatisfied. When complaints and criticisms have been used frequently, partners begin to expect to hear a list of things they haven't done or have done wrong. They come prepared to defend against those things and go into attack/deflect mode making it challenging to hear their partner's needs. When they are given a list of things they did that are valued instead, they feel seen and appreciated! When we acknowledge their values, priorities, and challenges people feel respected and it shifts the tone of the conversation, even when you are asking for change.

And rather than But

In the English language "and" joins two or more things together and "but" puts two or more things in contrast with one another. Many American English speakers use the word "but" in such a way as to negate positive things they have said to someone which breaks connection and increases relational conflict. For example, I love you but ... I appreciate your work but ... Using "but" in this way effectively erases those good things in the mind of the listener. It is essentially saying that "positive point a" is no longer true or is no longer relevant because of "negative point b". Two ways to fix this linguistically are to flip the order ("negative point b" but "positive point a") or use the word "and" instead.

For example:
- I love you *but* I am frustrated with our conversation. ("+ a" but "- b")
- I am frustrated with our conversation *but* I love you. ("- b" but "+ a")
- I love you *and* I am frustrated with our conversation. ("+ a" and "- b")
- I am frustrated with our conversation *and* I love you. ("- b" and "+ a")

As you read the examples notice in which sentence does "I love you" stand out the most? In which sentence does "I am frustrated with our conversation" stand out the most? Which sentence would you rather hear from a loved one? Which would feel the most connecting, rather than disconnecting? Despite being a one-word change, switching from but to and is often reported as one of the most challenging changes to make because we are so conditioned to say but!

A detailed request rather than criticism

When making requests from others it is very common to request the person to stop doing something or to tell them what you don't want or don't like. We frequently do this with children. We see this all the time in response to the best hopes question where clients are fully prepared to tell us all about what they don't want and when you ask what would they rather have they can really struggle to answer. A request to stop doing something or a complaint about what is or isn't happening typically leads to defensiveness and an argument, a pattern as old as time, and doesn't necessarily equate to what the person would rather be happening. In the same way that it is more productive to have a conversation with the client about what transformation they would like to achieve with services it is also far more productive and connecting for them to have a conversation with their partner about what they want and need, rather than offering a criticism or a complaint. This also means doing the work of figuring out what they want and need before going to their partner!

We also want details! When doing a preferred future description, we want all the details and those details are also important when making a request. One of the common complaints couples make is that they've told the other person what they want and it's not happening. Sometimes, they have only communicated part of what they want (without crucial details or have framed it in terms of what they don't want). People often assume that the details are obvious or that there is a "right way" that everyone knows about. They make a general request, for example, telling their partner they want to be acknowledged when they see each other at the end of the work day, and fail to include details such as a type, timeline, or the level of priority which can lead to conflict when the other person agrees to do the task but doesn't meet the unspoken need. Encouraging clients to share the details with one another helps to build mutual understanding. For example: "I want you to seek me out and give me a strong hug when we get home from work." Asking the other partner, "Did you know that is how they like to be hugged? What difference does it make to you to know that's what they are needing?" helps to draw their attention to the difference that providing details gives. When using these strategies couples often report feeling more loving towards their partner, being more aware of their partner, more patient, feeling more respected by their partner, and more valued for their contributions to the family.

Combining the parts of positive communication together makes the strongest impact and it is important to be mindful of how "but" or "and" will change the meaning of the communication. When we combine a *positive point a* with a *neutral or positive request* "and" makes an impact!

For example:
(Affirmation with a neutral request)
> Thank you for unloading the dishwasher <u>but</u> can you also load it.
> Thank you for unloading the dishwasher <u>and</u> can you also load it.

(Affirmation with a positive request)
> Thank you for unloading the dishwasher <u>but</u> I would really appreciate if you also loaded it.
> Thank you for unloading the dishwasher <u>and</u> I would really appreciate if you also load it.

As you read each of these example sentences think about how it would feel to hear the request. Which one leaves you feeling the most valued for your contribution? How does that impact how you receive their request? You can also try to formulate a positive communication request for someone in your life and ask them how it felt to receive the request in that way.

The difference receiving the request would make

The last part of positive communication is communicating why the the request is important to the asker and what difference it will make to receive it. "What difference will it make?" is a question we commonly ask clients because it gets to the meaning beyond the strategy. When we dig deeper into "what difference would it make" we often find core needs of support, safety, and connection. Communicating why something is important to you also helps the other person have a deeper understanding of your perspective and needs, helps them decide how to prioritize requests, and opens the possibility of getting to the difference in another way if the original request isn't possible for some reason. "No" is a legitimate response to any request, knowing why something is important to someone allows "no" to become "no, and". Successful relationships typically require reciprocal giving, compromise, and sacrifice. Deeply understanding your partners "why" and "difference" allows you to make more thoughtful decisions about when and how to give, compromise, and sacrifice.

Positive communication can be incredibly impactful even before it is even verbalized because one cannot help but experience a positive shift in perspective about the other person by thinking about and actively noticing what they have already done that is valued! It changes the words the person uses, impacts their tone of voice and body language, and makes them more open to hearing their partner. We often see this in session when we ask about how a couple met and what made them fall in love with each other. This shift is something we actively work to achieve with clients in session through our questions. Helping couples to learn how to do this themselves allows them be more intentional in their how the think about their partner and how they approach communicating their needs. Consider what difference it made to your practice as a solution focused clinician when you learned about using conditional presuppositions in your questions, such as using *when* rather than *if* when asking about future change (Froerer, Walker, & Lange, 2022; McGee, Vento, & Bavelas, 2005). Likely you were already using presuppositions some of the time. What difference did it make to have it brought to your attention and learning more about why it is helpful? Did you begin using it more often and with more intention? Couples who implement positive communication often report being more attentive to how they are communicating and having a significant decrease in arguments and miscommunications. They may also report a positive change in how they view and experience each other, feeling more like a team approaching challenges, feeling more valued in their relationship, and feeling more appreciation and love for one another.

References

de Shazer, S., Dolan, I., Korman, H., Trepper, T., McCollum, E., & Berg, I. K. (2012). *More than miracles: The state of the art of solution-focused brief therapy*. Routledge. Original work published in 2007)

Froerer, A. S., Walker, C. R., & Lange, P. (2022). Solution focused brief therapy presuppositions: A comparison of 1.0 and 2.0 SFBT Approaches. *Contemporary Family Therapy, 45,* 425-436. https://doi.org/10.1007/s10591-022-09654-5

McGee, D., Vento, A. D., & Bavelas, J. B. *(2005). An Interactional Model of Questions as Therapeutic Interventions. Journal of Marital and Family Therapy, 31*(4), 371-384. http://www.web.uvic.ca/psyc/bavelas/2005interact.pdf

Questions for the Reader

1. Paut, Vinay, and Angela practice as coaches and consultants as well as therapists. Coaches often take a more educational stance with their clients than therapists may do. How do Paut, Vinay, and Angela, in their different ways, and to differing extents, allow the client to remain the expert, even as they may be guiding their coaching or consultation clients?

2. How do each use solution focused skills differently in their work?

SOLUTION FOCUSED WORK AND CONFLICT RESOLUTION

Niki Lee Rowe
Marcos Perez LaMadrid

Niki Lee Rowe

Thirty plus years as a mediator has taught me to trust in mediation as the pathway to beneficial outcomes for those experiencing conflict. In 2016 through the Solution Focused Universe, I began to experience the value of applying a solution focused approach to the meditation process. As a therapist and mediator, I have had the opportunity to apply my skills from California to New York. As a New York Licensed Mental Health Counselor, I am also Certified with the National Board of Certified Counselors. I hold a certification in Anger Management Therapy and have with my solution focused team developed a Solution Focused Anger Management Program. I hold certifications in Conflict Resolution Coaching and Strategic Intervention Coaching. In California I was given the opportunity to administer Alzheimer's Facilities and acquired a certificate in Bio Medical Ethics. In 2008 My business partner and I published a national manual on 'Investigations in Long Term Care Facilities'. This chapter focuses on mediation and how the Solution Focused approach has matured that process and deepened the fulfillment I gain from experiencing my clients' outcomes.

What is your opinion of conflict? Most people regard it as negative, something to be avoided. From my perspective conflict equals opportunity. If two people always agree, then one of them is no longer necessary. Without differing thoughts and ideas there would be no innovation. Change can and does occur through well-handled conflict. The key rests in how to manage it. How do you personally 'do' conflict? Stop for a moment. Think about a time you were caught in a difference of opinion, maybe even an argument, and handled it really well. How did that feel? That's what mediation does. It sets the stage for that sense of accomplishment. Mediation brings two or more people together with a trained, neutral third party to work together toward a 'preferred future'. Does this sound like couples or family therapy? We don't call it therapy. But it can be therapeutic. At times people will not go to therapy because of the attached stigma. However, they will often come to mediation.

Any conflict can benefit from the mediation process. You've heard about it internationally regarding the avoidance of wars and you have heard of corporate mergers and agreements. The Humane Society and Sea World were an example of the beauty of two powers with a long-standing disagreement who grasped the opportunity to establish a partnership to save marine life for years to come while possibly saving the life of Sea World itself. Mediation can be used with divorcing couples fighting over custody of their children or finances and between parents and their unruly teenagers. It works with neighbors arguing over barking dogs. I've even mediated over the headstone a family wanted for their mother's grave, and believe this one, a dead chicken.

What brings people to mediation? 'Hope'. People come hoping for something better than they have been able to acquire so far. They hope to get 'un-stuck'. A good mediation makes the 'hoped-for' tangible. Once tangible, it can become real. A good mediator guides people in that transformation from hope to reality. As a mediator I guide participants in highlighting the details within the options they generate to achieve their 'preferred future'. As I have learned from Elliott Connie, I must be skilled in asking questions that produce meaningful responses.

I'm often asked why I have chosen to continue this work. Even after retiring from satisfying years as a therapist, mediation holds its place in my life and in my heart. I love the 'win-win.' This is where people come together to create a 'win' for everyone even though they may not know that at the beginning. This is not compromise. And, for myself, I never have to be the topic expert. The parties come with expertise regarding their issues and stories. The parties hold the content. I, as mediator, hold the process. My expertise is in creating safety and trust in the process. It is time for mediators to transition from the medical model of problem focused thinking. We need to learn to trust the people with whom we work. We need to let go of knowing the answers, teaching, giving advice and 'fixing' things for them. We must believe fully in the participants' capacity for change and in their abilities to construct their own lives. I come with the belief in their capability to reach their 'preferred future'.

This connection with people supports my desire to be of service during this retirement phase of my life. I share in conversations that transition people from the language of hurt to the language of hope. Detailing their hoped-for-future creates that future. They hear themselves speak the details of that future. They build their own solutions. People adhere to solutions they make themselves. My ideas may be fine for me, but they may not be fine for someone else. I don't know what will work for them. A judge can order 'solutions'. But a judge orders within the parameters of the court with no knowledge of these particular people. Individuals, however, can and do hold on to what is of their own making.

Participants reestablish relationships. Take the divorced couple. They will never be in love again. That's fine. Now they build a new life, a new way of working together for the benefit of their children and themselves. Often, I note to them a time 'dad' will be walking his daughter down the aisle. One second session began with my asking the husband "what's been better?" With a grimace he stated "nothing". The wife took a deep breath replying "gosh, I don't know about that." "Life with Johnny has been less stressful lately. Yesterday he told me, 'life is so much nicer now that you and dad can actually talk with each other'." That is my best hope. I hope they take the experience of this process into the future so they may never go back to court. Through the years it has been noted that even when no agreement happens, something for people changes often with an agreement coming about at a later time. If asked they often report that the mediation was successful.

Why have I incorporated Solution Focused work in this process? I'm not concerned about what got people to the mediation table. I don't ask. It can come up and be discussed as we work on future specifics. I care about where they want to go, that they detail how they will get there and can express what that will mean in their lives.

Early in my years as a mediator we were all generalists. We used one way of mediating. It worked. We mediated everything that came our way. Over the years, as with therapy, new models have evolved along with the requirement for mediators to have specialized trainings. All those models work. Yet, they tend to be problem-focused, coming from the belief that venting is necessary and that the mediator must hear all about the problem prior to working toward solutions. That does work. But solution focused conversations accomplish the task more often and more quickly. Once people become focused on the problem, they get lost in blaming and anger. The mediator becomes the referee with the need to turn them around towards their solutions. This takes time and hope diminishes. As angry emotions arise trust in the process and the hoped for outcome can be lost entirely.

What I want to do is help people 'find their way'. I come to every mediation with a stance that people not only can but will find their way. I believe in their capabilities. How? I sit in my soul with the presupposition of their capacity. My advice to mediators – 'hear them, not only with your head. Hear them with your heart.' Listen for where they want to go as you guide the process. Listen to their language. Using that, question them to find the resources they already own. Explore with them where and when the positives existed in the past. Help them remember. They came because something happened to change that once positive relationship. Exploring their history will remind them of what has worked and how they did that.

Case Example:

I did a mediation between a corporation and an independent consultant who had worked with the company for years. Now the consultant wanted his pay for the most recent project. They refused. Two men from corporate and the consultant entered the room and sat at the round table. Round helps to keep a balance of power in the room. The discussions became quite lively drawing security guards. However, with guidance they remembered the history of their past successes, such as why they always used this consultant, what it was about this company that brought him to trust and work with them over and over. The negatives disappeared in the positives. When we ask one person hope-filled questions and the history of the positives of the past relationship the others become elevated by hearing that. It makes them feel better. They left not only shaking hands, but agreeing on another project together and detailing how they would work together in the future in order to avoid misunderstandings. That's transformation. They not only found their solution, they also found their 'preferred future'. This is a great example of Barbara Fredrickson's 'Broaden and Build Theory' (Fredrickson,2004). When people feel positive emotion – their physical vision expands. Then their creative vision expands. Expanded creative vision means options that were not in mind before suddenly begin to come to mind.

Reflections

When I found Elliott Connie, Adam Froerer, and Solution Focused Brief Therapy in 2016 I became enamored. Before taking the second course I called Elliott and asked if there was anything more in this new course, and should I take it. He asked, "what are you hoping to get from it?" Obviously, I signed up. I have remained with them and Anna Francis and Cecil Walker on this never-ending journey of learning and maturing. Along the way I enlisted my good friend and mediation partner Dr. Bernadette Tracy. What we have found is that our success rate has risen tremendously while spending less time. Research shows that solution focused conversations have a positive effect in less time while satisfying the clients' need for autonomy. That's been true in my experience. In the recent world of virtual meetings, I am now given two hours per session with the goal of one to two sessions. The most I've needed recently is four. So, in the realm of Solution Focused Brief Therapy (SFBT), Solution Focused Mediation (SFM) is brief. No longer do I and the participants sit for hours.

Elliott Connie and Adam Froerer created the Diamond Approach to which I adhere. It fits perfectly with mediation as well as therapy. Transformation lives within the elements of the Diamond Approach. I have developed a mediation notes form to help the flow of the process during a session.

However, SF Mediation and SFBT do differ. SFBT allows for and expects change to take place 'after' the session. Mediation may have the same effect, but for mediation to be considered successful there must be a signed agreement. Here is the process.

The session begins, as with SFBT, asking everyone in the room to offer their own 'best hopes' from our work together. This is the formation of the 'desired outcome'. Even the lawyers in the room give me their 'best hopes'. I'm always amazed at how well that works and how energized they are to join in. Participants 'best hopes' are not the concrete goals or the positions on which they come. They are not where and when the children will be picked up or where they will stay on what weekend. 'Best hopes' is about 'why'. 'Best hopes' hold the underlying interests, the needs that generate the positions. "What difference will it make when the children are picked up on time." "What will that mean to you?" "I will be 'RELAXED, as I will know my children are safe". The 'best hopes' is the 'desired outcome', the underlying interest, the why they want the goal. We guide the way from positions to interests. We take their individual words and put them together in one productive whole. All these contributions get woven into an agreed upon 'desired outcome'. Here is a four-person example: 'best hopes' = comfort, good plan, joy, best possible father.

- "So, if you come away with a plan that offers comfort and joy in knowing you are the best parents you can be, would you be pleased?"

When everyone says 'yes', we have our first agreement. Now we all figuratively stand side by side working together toward their unified 'preferred future'. Now we know the difference these things will make for them.

We then go to the next phase which also diverges from SFBT. Everybody contributes to what they would like to accomplish today. Different than the 'best hopes,' these are the goals. These are the concrete items to be accomplished. We form a list and prioritize it with everyone's input. Now we have an agreed upon agenda. We now have two agreements, 1) our 'best hopes' and 2) our agenda.

Next, we move to the center of the Diamond to find the 'history of the outcome', their 'resources' and their resiliency. We do this with each item on their co-created agenda. I experience the beauty of the process as they detail not only how things worked in the past and how they did it, but how they use that revelation to detail the 'preferred future' for each of these items. Each one becomes another success and an experience of the work they will do together in the future.

I asked one divorced couple, "How did you meet?". He said, "in a bar". I then asked him the quintessential question "What was it about her that made you want to go talk with her?". His response, "she was the stripper!". All three of us burst out in laughter. "Then she leaned forward with, "yeah, and he was a really good tipper!". That is so much of what SF talk does. It lightens the mood. The process can become fun. People often let go of the pain and have a good laugh. They remember happiness. They are creating something new for themselves.

When they get stuck, hold the duality of the situation. This may be a situation that might never change. But their mindset can change. "Given that you are divorced and will need to be working on these issues as long as you are parenting together, what's your 'best hopes' from this conversation?"

As we work our way through the items on the agenda each becomes another agreement, another success along the journey. Each success opens the pathway to more successes. If we get stuck along the way, using the notes I'm keeping, I describe for them each of the individual agreements they have already made. Then they can choose to keep going or stop and set a time to come back. This is an emotional journey. If they choose to stop and come back or not the opportunity for change continues, as it does in SFBT, after or between sessions.

The requirement of writing an agreement adds an additional difference between SFBT and the mediation process. Success in mediation is predicated on ending with a completed and signed agreement. We write it together, detailing in their own words the agreements in each agenda item. The completed written agreement itself becomes the final mutual agreement, the evidence of their success. They sign it and take it to the courts or put it on their refrigerator to remind them of what they have accomplished.

Yes, this is different than SFBT in that we culminate with a written agreement. Or they may choose not to write an agreement. Yet, as with SFBT much transformation can happen outside of the session. I will never know. I must let go. This is all about them. When they come into the room, I assume they can and will do this. That stance appears contagious. My trust in them breeds trust in the process and trust in themselves. My hope is that the experience of this process lasts them a lifetime, agreement or not. In this process we experience 'Broaden and Build' and 'Hope Theory' wrapped into one. We widen possibilities and increase choices while expanding their availability to those possibilities. They take on the belief that they can do this.

The only mistakes the mediator can make are to stop co-constructing and start 'fixing' the problems. The one nonredeemable mistake happens if any of the participants get the perception the mediator has lost neutrality. So, as I continue to simply ask the next question and stay out of the way, they hear their own answers. Then, the beauty of the transformation becomes palatable.

Case Example: (The Lawyer, The Insurance Adjuster, and the Taxi Driver)

This case had been sitting on the desks of the attorney, John, and the insurance adjuster, Suzanne, for four years. They told me they had spent many frustrating meetings attempting to reach a resolution. Imagine the frustration for Javier, the owner of the New York City taxicab.

The accident itself had cost him a great deal and even more as he continued to wait for his insurance company to settle while his attorney fought to get him a satisfactory financial settlement.

This virtual mediation began with all three on Zoom with me. Alongside Javier stood his teenage son. Javier spoke little English. His computer skills were close to nonexistent. We began with my asking each of them for their 'Best Hopes' from our meeting. Who asks an attorney for their best hopes? Yet, the lawyer, and adjuster and Javier all were able to articulate the interests underlying their positions of "I want the money' and 'we have no adequate reasons to pay' to 'relief and success'. I asked, "So, if at the end of our meeting you find relief as you get this settled in a way that both you, John, and you, Suzanne, become successful and get this off both of your desks while satisfying your client's, Javier's, needs, would this have been successful for all of you?" I heard sighs of relief combined with a unanimous, 'yes'.

From this initial agreement we worked on and prioritized items for an agreed upon agenda. We then worked together through issues as to the insurance company's roadblocks and Javier's reasons for his steadfast demands. Suggestions were made by the participants as I would ask, "and, what difference would that make?" or "what would you want instead?", and other solution focused questions to help them expand their creativity and build their capacity for innovative suggestions. Javier's son translated and found documents in the computer for his dad. Then, in surprise, John asked if he could speak alone with Javier. My response, "of course". Zoom rooms are great. They returned and John announced, "we agree". "We think the offer from the insurance company is more than fair." A sigh of relief from everyone filled the virtual space.

Zoom's 'Share Screen' offers a wonderful way to collaborate. I sat back and typed as they agreed on the wording in their agreement. Everyone was satisfied. They had satisfied their goals and reached their 'desired outcomes'. Four years of arguing came to a close with a sigh of relief and more than a virtual smile from us all.

Here are my guidelines for successful solution focused mediations.

Guidelines:

THEME	PURPOSE	PROCESS

THEME	PURPOSE	PROCESS
What is Solution Focused Mediation?	Moving from win-lose or lose-lose outcomes to a win-win where all voices are honored and 'Best Hopes' can be achieved	1. Recognize each person's capacity for growth 2. Acknowledge differences in perspective 3. Use solution focused questioning to find underlying interests and weave them together for a common 'Desired Outcome' 4. Recognize the contributions of all

Solution Focused Mediation (SFM) resolves conflicts with a 'Preferred Future' focal point.	Mediation often occurs during a time of crisis, which offers an opportunity to come together utilizing a methodology for building capacity to employ differences as opportunities for common gain	Move from crisis to resolution - experiencing the process of solution building for a 'Preferred Future'
	Builds capacity for common interest construct	Gather the 'Best Hopes' of all involved
Mediator's 'Best Hopes'	Adversaries become allies learning while experiencing the collaborative process of working together for the benefit of all involved and those affected	Create the experience of the process as a formula for future work together
THEME	PURPOSE	PROCESS

LISTENING	• Participants become able to hear others' points of view and • Participants gain capacity to integrate the others' alternative points of view	• Listen for each person's language • Formulate questions based on each person's words
MOVING FROM POSITIONS TO INTERESTS	Participants move from WANTS (what I want) to NEEDS (interests)(why I need this)	• Ask questions to elicit 'Best Hopes' and weave them into the common interest statement • Construct questions based on the clients' language Example: "When….. is happening, what difference will it make?"
THEME	PURPOSE	PROCESS

THEME	PURPOSE	PROCESS
QUESTIONING	Participants move from problem focused discussion to discussion focused on the 'Desired Outcome' through use of the DIAMOND - 'History of the Outcome', 'Resources', 'Preferred Future' Participants' change in mindset begins	Use the client's language to stimulate brain plasticity through Solution Focused questioning
THE SOLUTION FOCUSED SEQUENCE	<u>Mediator Introduces</u> the mediation process to begin establishing safety and trust	• Detail the process • Answer all questions re the mediation • Create trust

THEME	PURPOSE	PROCESS
	<u>"Best Hopes"</u> Mediator establishes each persons 'Best Hopes' through questioning for their underlying needs/interests	• Gather each individual's 'Best Hopes' from this work together • Dig for the meaning that these accomplishments will bring in their lives
	Mediator forms and gathers agreement on a combined 'Best Hopes' statement to create a unified focus for the mediation	• Combine everyone's 'Best Hopes' into one common ground statement • Note this accomplishment as their first agreement

THEME	PURPOSE	PROCESS
	<u>Agenda/Goals</u> The agenda is inclusive of all participants wishes, including the court or other outside authority	• With the participants gather agreement on items to accomplish • With participants prioritize items and create the agenda focused on accomplishing the participants' and the court's
	<u>Use of The Diamond</u> • Solution Focused conversation creates each agenda item as the chance to become another agreement • Each agreement creates continual expansion of hope and creative thought	• Mine for 'Resources', 'History of the Outcome', • 'Detail the 'Preferred Future'

THE SOLUTION FOCUSED AGREEMENT	ASK, GATHER, GENERATE, AND CREATE	
	<ul><li>Opportunity for more collaboration</li><li>Participants collaborate on wording and assure they are in agreement on each item</li></ul>	Write the agreement in conjunction with the participants, using their language
CLOSING THE SESSION	Opportunity to acknowledge, thank, encourage	<ul><li>Offer the opportunity to return for another session to finish if necessary</li><li>Offer the opportunity to return to mediation if future items arise</li><li>Thank them for the honor of working with them.</li><li>Goodbye</li></ul>

Inside the co-constructed conversation, we discover the broadening of ideas and the emerging of new mindsets. I offer this to all mediators, recognize that we hold the process. The clients hold the content. We are not the experts of their lives. I offer the advice to center yourself before your mediation. Come to the people you will be guiding and share the space they offer. See them as the heroes they are in their own lives. Begin your time with them by asking for their 'desired outcome' from this time together and what it will mean in their lives. What they need from this experience is more important than the problem that brought them to you. Help them discover their strengths and resources. Help them remember the history of how they have generated positive outcomes in the past. Guide them in using all those revelations to detail their 'preferred future', the future where everyone will be benefiting. Be free to laugh with them when the memories of good times from the past arise.

Mediation for me remains as fulfilling and beautiful as ever. Solution Focused Mediation has given me the opportunity to continue to join with people on their journeys even more deeply. It allows me to be of service while continually growing and living my own 'preferred future'. To all mediators I offer that as you transition to Solution Focused work you will find the joy that comes from this never-ending journey of deepening and maturing our learning, our understanding, and our acceptance of others and of ourselves. Yes, this is hard work. And, yes, this is truly heart work.

References:

1.	Fredrickson BL. "The broaden-and-build theory of positive emotions." (2004) *Philos Trans R Soc Lond B Biol Sci. Sep 29;359(1449):1367-78.* doi: 10.1098/ rstb.2004.1512. PMID: 15347528; PMCID: PMC1693418.

Marcos Perez LaMadrid

In Bolivia the indicators of violence are concerning. According to the Gender Observatory, in 2020 between March and May 2,935 cases of violence were registered. Between January and September of the same year, 86 cases of femicide, the intentional killing of individuals based on gender, were reported. These incidences are causing Bolivian society and institutions to activate different mechanisms in an effort to eradicate violence. As a solution-focused therapist, I am interested in helping to eradicate violence by doing something different and useful.

I am presently in a creative and inductive stage of my research and intervention. I work at the Universidad Mayor de San Andrés (UMSA), where I coordinate a program that strengthens family protection services in rural areas. I am investigating how the Solution Focused Approach (SFA) works in Bolivia and within the family protection arena. This chapter shows how I frame my work, the lessons I've learned trying to incorporate the SFA, and also proposes what guidelines connect the SFA with the culture of peace. The chapter also includes an example of a solution-focused conversation in the multicultural context of Bolivia.

Table 1 summarizes my experience in violence prevention work in rural communities in Bolivia.

Table 1: SFA in Bolivian Rural Communities-A Framework.

From the Solutions Approach	Peace Culture
Ask questions	Decolonization
Desired outcome	Positive peace notion of well-being of the person in their culture.
Description of presence of desired outcome	Cultural portability
Use of language	Willingness to communicate
Presuppositions and constant change	Community resources

Ask = Decolonization

I visit communities accompanied by UMSA students. I am interested in talking with people in the communities and, like any solution-focused therapist, I try to ask questions that promote hope. I see this as a decolonizing action, understanding that having these conversations is one way to deconstruct power. I do not go to the communities to diagnose cultures or to tell them how they should live, but rather, as a visitor who listens and is ready to ask the next question, thus keeping the individuals and groups in the position of power within the relationship.

Desired Outcome = Positive Peace Notion of Well-being of the Person in Their Culture.

Asking about the desired outcome or the desired transformation people want in their lives helps me to know what the person's notion of well-being is within their own community. These desired outcomes may include internalized states (emotions), ways of interacting with others, and ways of relating to nature. I ask questions like, What are your best hopes?, or directly inject the idea of peace by asking: If tomorrow there was a consistent peace in your community, how would you notice it? The first question leads people to directly develop their notion of well-being, and the second question leads them to describe their own notion of community peace.

The ideas of Culture of Peace help explain the elegance of the SFA, because through simple conversations it generates action-oriented participation in communities. The United Nations (1998, Resolution A/52/13) defines a Culture of Peace as a series of values, attitudes and behaviors that reject violence and prevent conflicts by trying to attack their causes in order to solve problems through dialogue and cooperation. negotiation between people, groups and nations (https://www.un.org/en/ga/62/plenary/peaceculture/bkg.shtml), but, through the lens of SFBT, I appreciate the idea that there is negative peace and positive peace. Negative peace is when you only talk about what you do not want, which would be associated with the problem (Calderón, 2009). To maintain negative peace, authorities that control and punish are needed, their benefits are short-term, but it is not maintained over time because the community is passive. On the other hand, positive peace is when you work to promote the presence of what you want; this would fit very well with the solution focused approach, which invites you to use a language of the presence of the solution and not of the absence of the problem (Ercoskun, 2021). Its effects would be in the medium and long-term, and would be long-lasting because positive peace is dependent on community management.

Description of the Presence of Desired Outcome = Cultural Portability

Magic happens when individuals or groups are asked questions about the presence of their desired results or the sense of well-being in their lives. Each answer they provide contains unique details forged in the language they use that is specific to their community. These conversations provide great cultural portability because the conversation offers a series of invitations to action in a respectful and realistic way according to the worldview of each person within their own culture.

Use of Language = Willingness to Communicate

Perhaps the essence of this magic is the therapist's disciplined use of the client's language. Each word acquires its meaning within the conversation and not in the dictionary. The language of the indigenous communities I work with is Aymara. The Spanish language is a secondary language. This does not stop me because I   consider that in each conversation a new language is created based on linguistic calibrations that are co-constructed. Typically people who are in this field of fighting against violence use the language of an expert and a description of the problem, which means investigating the causes of violence and developing a diagnosis of the culture. I, on the other hand, direct these conversations towards the prevention of violence and therefore I prefer to presuppose community resources that allow the descriptions of positive peace to come true.

Patterns that Connect

I find the patterns that connect the SFA and the Culture of Peace is the "Design of Peace", which is defined as the description of positive peace fed by the notion of well-being in the lives of people in their culture, which would enable the activation of community resources (https://www.un.org/en/ga/62/plenary/peaceculture/bkg.shtml). This means that the more descriptions of this type, the greater the provocation for collaborative change while respecting cultural diversity.

The following example shows an excerpt from the session with Anita, who expresses that her desired outcome for the session is peace and tranquility. I, as a therapist, ask questions about the preferred future so that Anita can describe what her life would be like with peace and tranquility. These concepts, in themselves, describe Anita's own notion of well-being within her cultural and social environment.

(In Spanish in the region where Marcos lives, the words calm and tranquility have the same meaning. The words relief and peace also have the same meaning).

> Marcos: Imagine tomorrow you wake up calmer and relieved, how would you notice?
>
> Anita: I would like to go for a walk, I like to walk quietly and go to clear my head.

Marcos: Where would you walk tomorrow?

Anita: Through Villa Fátima to walk there, a place by the summit. I can go eat some fish there.

Marcos: Wow, walk to the top, near the top and eat some fish over there?

Anita: Yes, I like to go there for the peace, the tranquility.

Marcos: What would the beginning of your path be like in that place?

Anita: Yes, I would have to take a bus and just start my walk.

Marcos: Yeah. and when you arrive and start your walk. What would you notice around you if you are calmer and more relieved?

Anita: I am a country person and I do not like cities.

Marcos: Um hmm.

Anita: Quiet places give me a lot of peace.

Marcos: When you are starting your walk-through Pongo, with this tranquility, with this relief, what things would you find, what things would catch your attention?

Anita: The landscape.

Marcos: What part of the landscape would catch your attention?

Anita: The hills.

Marcos: The hills?

Anita: The hills, the color of nature is what I love to see the most.

Marcos: Did you say the color or the smell of nature?

Anita: Yes, when you go to the field there are some very nice colors.

Marcos: What colors would you see tomorrow if you are at peace, perhaps walking through Pongo, beginning to walk, quietly?

Anita: The colors, the first thing I would see is the sky, the color blue and light blue, at this time they are very beautiful.

Marcos: What difference would it make tomorrow if you saw these blue and light blue colors in the sky as you started walking?

Anita: Difference to what it is now?

Marcos: Yes, what would be special at that moment, when you see these blue and light blue colors in the sky tomorrow?

Anita: The difference would be the tranquility being there. That would be the difference to where I am now.

Marcos: What else would happen tomorrow?

Anita: That I would like many good things to happen tomorrow, above all.

Marcos: And while you would be walking, what else would happen tomorrow?

Anita: What else would happen? I don't know, maybe I'd like to see animals along the way.

Marcos: What animals would you see tomorrow on your journey?

Anita: Vizcachas, bears. I would like to see that.

Marcos: How would you react tomorrow if you were seeing these animals? Seeing these colors? What would be different? What would be special in the way you walked while you were there?

Anita: Well, I would feel happy, calm, something special.

Marcos: Happy, calm. Perhaps there would be someone else who could notice? Someone close to you? That you are this way, calm in peace?

Anita: Someone... well... I don't know... since I live alone.

Marcos: Of course you live alone. And I don't know what you think about this question, if the mountains could see you calm, relieved, in peace, while you walk there, how would the mountains realize that you are calm and relieved and in peace?

Anita: I would be looking at them. I think, maybe I would talk to them.

Marcos: What would you say to the mountains, to the hills?

Anita: I would give them compliments about having very pretty rock shapes.

Marcos: What would they answer you?

Anita: What would they answer me?

Marcos: Yes

Anita: Let's see. I don't know. A joke has occurred to me. I don't know what they would tell me. Maybe they would tell me, "Not you.". (both laugh)

Marcos: They would tell you something like a joke, "You don't look good", like a joke?

Anita: Yes.

Marcos: And how would you respond?

Anita: With another joke. (she laughs)

Marcos: What would you tell them? More or less.

Anita: Let's see, I don't know. I like to laugh. I would have a very pleasant talk with them with laughter.

Marcos: Wow! A very pleasant chat with laughter, with jokes between you and the mountains. And how would heaven notice that you are relieved and at peace?

Anita: Well what I see is that the sky would notice that I'm happy. (laughs) Because he would see that I am enduring the weather.

Marcos: Aha. That you are enduring the sun and stuff?

Anita: Yes.

Marcos: And what would heaven think of you?

Anita: Sure would be happy. Because in the city I am hiding from the sun. Then he would know.

Marcos: And what would he tell you?

Anita: I don't know, he would tell me that I am burning or toasting. (laughs)

Marcos: And what would you say to heaven?

Anita: I would tell him that I am happy and content.

Marcos: Has this peace and quiet been happening before?

Anita: Yes

In the example above I am concentrating on using the client's language, he is also constantly calibrating (confirming and adapting) my questions so the client understands them and flows in her responses. It should be noted that everything flows more when both co-construct the conversation with an animist language that describes Anita's interaction with the sky, the colors and the mountains.

For me, it is a total privilege to know Anita's vision of the world and to share it in this text. I consider that the solution-focused approach allows us to generate more than linguistic bridges, it allows us to connect in a unique and transformative way that is visible in each conversation.

References

Arslan , Havva & Turhan , Yunus. (2016). Reconciliation-oriented Leadership: Nelson Mandela and South Africa. All Azimuth: A Journal of Foreign Policy and Peace. 5. 29-29. 10.20991/allazimuth.257676.

Ercoskun , Burak . (2021). On Galtung's Approach to Peace Studies. Leto Socialis 5(1), pp. 5-7

Calderón Concha, Percy (2009). Johan Galtung's conflict theory. Peace and Conflict Magazine, (2), 60-81. [Consultation date June 27, 2022]. Available at: https://www.redalyc.org/articulo.oa?id=205016389005

Gender Observatory Bolivia (2020). Facts and figures on gender violence. http://www.coordinadoradelamujer.org.bo/observatorio/index.php/datoscifras/all

United Nations (1998). RESOLUTION APPROVED BY THE GENERAL ASSEMBLY on Culture of Peace. Resolution A/52/13 in 1998. www.unesco.org/cp/uk/uk_sum_refdoc.htm

Questions for the Reader:

1. Niki and Marcos work in different cultural contexts, and each has adapted to the legal and economic systems where they are. How do you adapt to the cultural background of your clients?

2. Both Niki and Marcos work to reduce violence. How might a solution focused approach help reduce violence in the cases you see?

SOLUTION FOCUSED THERAPY IN THE TREATMENT OF ADDICTIONS

Melanie Bray *(outpatient addictions treatment)*

Melanie Bray

Addiction does not discriminate—it can ravage the lives of anyone regardless of education, socioeconomic status, race, culture, religion, and sexual orientation, etc. I had this realization as a social work student during one of my initial practicums at an addiction agency. This humbling experience increased my empathy and ability to practice from a non-judgmental stance. I remember hearing so many stories of trauma and suffering. For many of the folks I encountered, substance use had become a means of coping with and/or escaping their traumatic memories, flashbacks, and other distressing thoughts and feelings.

During my initial practicum—which turned into an offer of employment—I was trained to ask questions that explored and determined the 'root cause(s)' of addiction. I was 'indoctrinated' to believe that discovering the origins of addiction would lead to the development of appropriate and effective treatment plans. I recall having one such exploratory conversation with an initial client, "Jim" (name changed for reasons of confidentiality) —early thirties and struggling with alcohol dependence. Despite overturning every stone I could think of to find a root cause, we struggled to discover anything—other than he really loved the taste of alcohol! Embarking on a 'dissection' of Jim's childhood, I learned his mother had a very serious mental illness. As a youth Jim's life had been chaotic and unpredictable. I concluded that such instability in Jim's childhood led to problematic drinking. As I reflect on the conclusion I made approximately 19 years ago, it now seems very arrogant, possibly incorrect, and unhelpful. How does parent-blaming lead to a meaningful intervention plan?

Other cringe-worthy moments include telling clients, "Things will get *worse* before they get better." This was a popular statement when I entered the field of social work. Many colleagues using problem-focused approaches (me included) received feedback from clients that they felt worse upon entering therapy. Can you imagine? Reaching out to a therapist at a time in our lives when we feel defeated, deeply distressed, and possibly at our lowest point, only to discover that the therapeutic process can amplify these feelings! Sadly, I think the purpose of this statement is two-fold: 1) to reassure clients that the increased distress felt at the start of therapy is normal; 2) to encourage clients to hang in and resist the natural urge to quit something that is causing increased distress. Interestingly, after specializing in SFBT, I can't remember the last time I heard a client report feeling worse at the beginning of our work together. I am much more likely to hear enthusiasm and eagerness for the next session. The insecure and self-conscious part of me worries I won't be able to live up to this expectation and recreate the 'magic' clients frequently describe from the first session— and I'm okay with this! I think this is a much better place to be than feeling guilty or worried about clients' mental/ emotional well-being after they leave my office!

Another thing that stands out to me from my early years is the level of details clients provided about their substance(s) of choice: how a particular substance feels, tastes, smells, looks, method of delivery, etc. In the addiction treatment community where I work, such descriptions have been referred to as "glorifying the substance." Glorifying substance use is typically viewed in a negative light because it can trigger such strong cravings that a client is more likely to seek out and use after the counseling session. As I've developed more confidence conducting SFBT conversations, I rarely encounter this phenomenon today. I believe this is a result of the approach. I think it is difficult to provide detailed descriptions of substances while engaging in conversations that explore desired outcomes and preferred futures—these things become incongruent or incompatible. Nowadays, my clients are less likely to report cravings during sessions and more often describe themselves as feeling inspired, hopeful, and having a greater commitment to their desired outcome. In fact, I have come to view in-session cravings as a sign of a possible misstep. Perhaps in that instance I veered off the solution-focused course and dipped into the problem focused waters.

As you can imagine, hearing endless stories of detailed substance use and traumatic experiences at the very start of my career led to depression and burn-out. After a mere eight months, I submitted my resignation—harboring the belief I was 'too sensitive' and 'not cut out' for the addictions field. Turning to the education system, I became a School Social Worker. Several years into this role, I applied to graduate school. While taking a course on individual therapy, I was introduced to an approach called Solution Focused Brief Therapy. There was something absolutely fascinating (and relieving) about the modality's recognition of the client as expert of their own life. I was also struck by the lack of focus on client deficits and pathology. I felt excitement and curiosity bubbling up. Shortly after graduation, I enrolled in a SFBT certificate program through the University of Toronto, Canada—I was hooked!

Five years after I started practicing SFBT, I returned to my roots in addiction counseling. I always felt I had 'unfinished business.' Maybe I had something to prove to myself – or perhaps it was my calling. Regardless of the reason, what I do know with certainty is SFBT saved my career and made me a better therapist. Many colleagues have playfully accused me and my clients of "having too much fun" during sessions. This is a reference to the laughter that is often heard emanating from my office. I also tend to go through fewer tissue boxes!

Harm Reduction Model

The addiction agency I work for endorses a harm reduction model. This approach or stance entails accepting where the client is at (i.e., current level of substance use) and the changes they would like to make. When utilizing a harm reduction approach, therapists do not pressure/expect clients to choose a goal of abstinence and we accept whatever reductions clients wish to make. For example, I worked with a teenager who used cocaine 4-5 times per week and wanted to limit her use to occasional weekends. Even though this substance is illegal in Canada—and one might have many other reasons for wanting a teenager to avoid cocaine—being client-centered and working from a harm reduction model required me to accept whatever goal the client set. Fortunately, most of my clients revise their original harm reduction goals, typically opting for total abstinence or some other version of extreme reduction. I attribute these frequent goal revisions to SFBT. As clients start to experience the preferred futures they describe in session, the more enticing and attainable these become. It's like sampling a delicious morsel and wanting more—a little taste is not enough.

I worked with a young adult, Shane (not his real name), who wanted to reduce his alcohol consumption to the level of his peers. Whenever Shane attended a pub with friends, he was typically onto his third beer before anyone else had finished their first round. Shane often drank to the point of blacking out. In the days that followed such black-outs, embarrassing incidents were threaded together for him by family members, peers, and tiny memory fragments. Convincing Shane to pursue a goal of abstinence at the start of our work would have felt alienating and insurmountable. As therapy progressed, Shane managed to avoid drinking on weeknights. However, he soon realized that it was nearly impossible for him to stop drinking once he started, so he revised his goal. He became more selective about friends. He placed more trust in his moods/emotions to help him decide if/when he could attend social gatherings in 'high-risk' settings. When Shane announced he was ready to complete therapy, he was completely abstaining from alcohol, had his driver's license reinstated, and was accepting extra shifts at work to save money for school!

My workplace collects the following data during each counseling session: 1) most recent substance use; 2) amount of last use; 3) average use since the previous session. I am not a fan of this practice because it feels incongruent with SFBT. I believe this line of inquiry is intrusive and can leave clients feeling shamed and judged. There continues to be much stigma surrounding addiction and mental health. Many clients are embarrassed to admit they are consuming 12 or more drinks daily or using crystal meth multiple times a day. I also believe there is no therapeutic link between disclosing quantity of use and achieving desired outcomes. Regardless of these reservations, my agency tried to reassure me that such data collection creates a level of accountability for the client. How can we be sure of this assumption? And why am I deemed the person to instill accountability?

To illustrate my beliefs, I would like to share Brian's story (not his real name). Brian was a graduate student in his late twenties. At the time of our meeting, Brian was using cocaine, alcohol, and cannabis. Based on information Brian shared, he consumed alcohol and cannabis daily and alluded to cocaine use on weekends. I did not press further for exact frequency and quantity. In less than eight months, Brian quit using alcohol and cocaine and proceeded to set a goal of abstinence for cannabis! This was a huge shift from Brian's initial goal: to abstain from cocaine. While reflecting on Brian's amazing progress during our final session, he casually referred to using cocaine daily when he first reached out to our agency. Keeping my stunned reaction internalized, I reflected on this disclosure. It confirmed/ validated my belief: knowing the exact amounts and frequency of substance use is not an indicator or predictor of client success/outcome. I also want to add, during the years I have been applying SFBT in addiction work, nearly every client has expressed gratitude for my non-judgmental stance. Because SFBT doesn't require collection of amounts/frequency of substance use to facilitate conversations about change, clients can maintain their dignity and feel less embarrassed in session—in the process feeling non-judged.

Brian put a great deal of effort into reducing (and ultimately abstaining from) alcohol and cocaine. During this process, I frequently asked Brian what differences he noticed each time a reduction was made. Brian described wonderful improvements: increased energy, memory, clarity, creativity, motivation, focus, interest, and attention. The young man who initially presented as lethargic and bored was transforming into a passionate and excited version of himself! He started to care deeply about his health, studies, and collaborating with mentors in his field.

As Brian neared the end of our work together, his name eventually rose to the top of a long waitlist for trauma therapy at a reputable agency. In one of our final sessions, Brian looked crestfallen as he recounted the concerns his new trauma therapist expressed.

The new therapist worried Brian was merely substituting alcohol and cocaine for school/work demands. Brian began doubting himself—had he simply replaced one addiction for another? Or was he using school/work as a distraction from deeper unresolved issues? The trauma therapist also expressed concerns about the speed at which Brian was tapering cannabis use. She was fearful of a monumental relapse if this final substance was removed too quickly from Brian's life.

I was disheartened to learn that Brian's new therapist questioned his school workload and harm reduction plan. When I worked with Brian, he successfully developed, implemented, and revised every aspect of his harm reduction plans. Questioning Brian's recovery at this late stage felt dismissive of his efforts and values that emerged over the past eight months. It also seemed to discount the excitement and joy he felt about his new commitments and healthy lifestyle.

It appears the trauma therapist's line of questioning is indicative of mainstream problem-focused approaches. One can imagine her listening for cognitive distortions and maladaptive behaviors. Naturally, a therapist with this orientation would make inquiries about substitution behaviors and distracting oneself with high workload demands to avoid 'underlying' or 'unresolved issues.' What a contrast from the types of questions a SFBT therapist might pose:

1. How did you manage to abstain from alcohol and cocaine in less than eight months?
2. How did you decide it was a good idea to set a goal of abstinence for cannabis?
3. How did you know this was the right time to start this tapering plan?
4. How did you develop this plan?
5. What does it say about you, developing your own tapering plan and seeing it come to fruition?
6. What differences have you already noticed?
7. What's been different because of committing to more school/work projects?
8. How do you manage to balance your workload demands and enjoy the process?
9. What difference does it make when you engage mindfully in your school/work demands? Or What

differences do you notice when you catch yourself mindfully engaged in your school/work demands?
10. What do you know about yourself that reassures you can balance all these projects and heavy workload?

While sharing Brian's story, I was overwhelmed with gratitude for those in the SFBT field who introduced, taught, mentored, and showed me another way of practicing. Problem-focused approaches teach therapists to search for client's problem-areas and deficits. Once clients are sufficiently pathologized and have their deficits brought to awareness, therapist and client can begin the arduous task of rebuilding and learning how to think and behave differently. With SFBT, we are gifted a line of inquiry that highlights (in the very first session!) what clients are already doing well and we get to co-construct detailed descriptions of who/what clients want to become. Clients immediately start feeling inspired and motivated—and we have the privilege of witnessing their transformation right before our very eyes! I cannot imagine practicing drug and alcohol counseling without SFBT. I love this modality's capacity for unearthing even the most subtle and minute improvements people make while reducing their use.

I am hard-pressed to recall a client who has not made any efforts to change their use before attending the first appointment. I have even more difficulty recalling anyone who hasn't taken steps toward their desired outcome between the first and second session. Unfortunately, many clients attending therapy have been given ultimatums and/or pressured to quit using altogether. It can be quite discouraging to the client, and their loved ones, when abstinence is not achieved overnight. SFBT thus becomes a protective factor and form of relapse prevention in and of itself. Because this modality invites us to explore differences and improvements in such fine detail (regardless of type or size), clients remain motivated and inspired to continue with their efforts.

For example, I remember attending a case conference and hearing a client proudly announce having three days of abstinence. The attending physician nonchalantly stated, "It's only been three days." I could feel the air rushing out of the room as my client winced and hung his head. I quickly jumped in and asked the client if avoiding alcohol for three days was a little or big surprise. The client said this was the first time in years he did "not have a drop of alcohol for three days in a row." When I asked how he managed to do this, a smile crept across his face, and he sat a little taller in his chair.

Not only does SFBT unearth and magnify the most minute changes/improvements, but it is also well equipped to handle the impossible! Non-SF therapists at times claim that the modality is superficial—that it cannot be used as an intervention for really difficult problems. No one debunks this myth better than Seraphina. Seraphina's real name has been changed to protect her privacy. I chose this name because it means "ardent and fiery," words I would use to describe this mother of two!

During the pandemic, I received a referral for a young woman who worked as a prison guard. In our first session, Seraphina said connecting with the agency was the culmination of a recent workplace incident and her husband's insistence that she quit drinking. In subsequent sessions, I learned Seraphina was bombarded by rumors about her struggles with alcohol and that she was subjected to racist and sexist comments every time she set foot in the prison. As rumors flew, friends quickly became foes, and consequently, some postings grew very dangerous. Critical incidents—which require immediate attention—were being met with hesitancy and intentionally delayed responses, oftentimes leaving Seraphina without assistance or back-up. Attending critical incidents alone, even for a moment, could be life-threatening.

The more I learned about Seraphina's toxic workplace, the more I became curious about her strength and resilience. How did Seraphina manage to work in this prison setting for so many years despite facing overt and covert racism/sexism? How did she manage to continue working after the incident— as opposed to taking a leave of absence? Even though Seraphina admitted alcohol had become a way of coping with workplace toxicity, personal grief, loss, and trauma, I continued to express awe and wonderment at her tenacity and desire for change. In response to these questions, Seraphina described her thought processes and actions that resulted in such determination and persistence. During one of these exploratory conversations, Seraphina expressed a desire to be more like one of her female colleagues who seemed to 'fly under the radar.' I invited Seraphina to give a detailed description of what she noticed about her colleague.

In our next session, I asked Seraphina the traditional SFT follow-up question: "What's been better?" Seraphina proceeded to discuss ways in which she was adopting her colleague's presentation and posture. As the weeks progressed, Seraphina excitedly reported that the rumors about her were lessening, colleagues were showing more respect, and she was gaining confidence. Seraphina said she was "holding [her] head up high" and becoming less concerned about colleagues' opinions! This was coming from a woman who previously went out of her way to befriend coworkers and constantly worried what they thought of her! Seraphina also reported a significant reduction in alcohol consumption because she was coping better. When asked about this transformation, Seraphina said she turned her thoughts to her husband and children—because family is what matters most to her. Seraphina redirected her attention and efforts to staying safe in a dangerous workplace so her children will be able to grow up with a mother.

We have often heard as Solution Focused practitioners that this approach is "problem-phobic." I completely disagree with this. When Seraphina shared her experiences of systemic racism, sexism, and traumatic grief/loss, I did not interrupt or ignore her problem descriptions. For me personally, in the retelling of the problem story lies gold! That is when I'm carefully and deliberately listening for resilience, strengths, times when the client stands up to or resists the problem, and occasions when the client does something different and/or instead of using substances. In this way, SF work is also attuned to issues of social justice and context.

Questions for the Reader:

1. Melanie describes "cringe worthy" experiences with therapeutic approaches which did not work for her and her clients. Have you had similar experiences?

2. How does Melanie's solution focused approach convey acceptance and empathy to her clients?

SOLUTION FOCUSED THERAPY IN SOCIAL WORK AND FAMILY PRESERVATION

Greg Oberbeck *(community mental health and suicide prevention)*

Greg Oberbeck

I began my career with a flight into the unknown, and this adventurous spirit has informed my work ever since. Graduating with a master's degree in social work from the University of Missouri – Kansas City, an opportunity arose to live and work in the United Kingdom – where I had never been. It sounded like a good idea, so I took a chance and went to England on a six-month student visa – 18 years ago. I worked for several years in different roles with teenagers leaving the care system and then a different team triaging referrals into Social Care. While I enjoyed the roles, I wouldn't say I had really found my passion, something was missing. It wasn't until I landed a job working as a senior social worker in a family preservation service that I really felt that spark. This was also my first introduction to solution focused work, as the service was dedicated to utilizing the approach as its main methodology.

I remember the moment it happened. As the service was just being developed, I didn't have a full case load to work with, so my manager told me to go and read some books on the solution focused approach while I had the time. And I remember reading a book called Brief Coaching: A Solution Focused Approach by Chris Iveson, Evan George and Harvey Ratner. I remember going through those pages, seeing the conversations in the book and hearing about the changes that took place for people, and that was it. I thought to myself, 'yes, this is exactly why I got into social work in the first place!' With my excitement riding high, I could not wait to start applying this in my work.

Then the reality of working within a vast, complex system hit. My initial introduction to family preservation work was overwhelming. For both social worker and client, the system has its own agenda, its own way of working and its own challenges to navigate. The services are defined as completely voluntary, and yet the client constantly worries that refusal to participate can and will be held against them by the child welfare authorities. There have also been times where a referral to the family preservation service is made and must be explored before looking at any other options for support. Beyond the system itself there was then the harsh realities of my clients' lives – poverty, chaos, multiple traumas, and the involvement of authorities who often seemed to make things more challenging rather than being helpful.

My excitement about solution focused work was still there, however, I had those inklings of doubt. How on earth could this seemingly simple approach make a difference in the midst of everything that my clients had to deal with? Would these questions make a difference? It will be no surprise to you to hear that solution focused work was a lifeline for me as a practitioner and for my clients. Solution focused work allowed me to ask questions about hope and what my clients wanted. It was different for all of us, and yet a question about hopes and what it was they wanted from the work somehow seemed to lift them above the fog of everything that wasn't going well or that they were told they were doing wrong and give them sight of the family life that they wanted. This was of course reinforced when the family would talk about what was already working and going well for them. They were now looking and focusing on their own strengths and carving out a hopeful path to the life they were after.

While there have been several moments over the years that have been significant learning points for me, there is one in particular I want to share with you. It happened back in 2014 while I was studying for my solution focused diploma from BRIEF in London. I was as eager as you could be, confidence was high. I was ready to take on anything. I had a family referred to me where the mother, Lucy, had eight children, aged from 6 up to 21, and Lucy had already been widowed twice. She had had negative experiences with therapy and a variety of other professionals, and yet she agreed for me to come and visit. This was done with a polite manner that somehow also sent a message of skepticism, almost as if saying, 'here comes another professional, let's see what you're going to do.'

When we start, we sat down in her home, I had my notebook out ready to write things down so I could document the conversation for the agency. I even had questions and prompts for questions written in the margins of my notebook. I was ready, or so I thought. I asked Lucy, 'what are your best hopes from our work together?' She looked at me in disbelief. 'Hope? What do you mean hope?' she fired back. I repeated my question to which she then proceeded to tell me about all of the challenges she is facing as a mother, the concerns she had for her children, how her partners had passed away, the impact that this had on her and the floodgates had opened.

I checked my notebook, tried my questions and various versions of a 'best hopes' question. She kept telling me her story. I tried to acknowledge what she was telling me and get back to a question. It wasn't enough. She kept telling me more and more about the years of struggle and challenge that they had been through. We weren't connecting. Then it hit me. I thought to myself, 'Greg, shut up and listen.' And so I stopped thinking about SF structures or anything related to a list of questions or techniques. I sat, and I listened. About 40 minutes later, Lucy finished what she had wanted to tell me about her story. And I remember being absolutely filled with the weight of everything that she had been through and having only one possible question that I could ask her, 'how in the heck are you still here and sitting on this couch in front of me?"

Lucy instantly started to cry. She said that no one had ever asked her that before. She talked about how every other professional always tried to tell her how brave she was, how amazing she was and how strong she was – but she didn't feel any of those things. She talked about being a fighter and how she would do anything she possibly could for her children. We stopped there, and she agreed to see me again.

We had a handful of sessions after that, some with several of the children present, and you can imagine what we covered. In that second session it was Lucy and her daughter, and we explored their hopes and what that might look like for them. I still remember them talking about the music that would be on the radio and how they'd be singing along together. After that we explored what's been better and worked through blips and things that came up. By the end things weren't perfect, but they were all much happier, Lucy's daughter was back in school, and her behavior had improved there and at home. The family was working together and living in a way that worked for them, and thankfully it also worked for the professionals around them.

Lucy and her family taught me the importance of listening, and I mean genuinely listening to connect with someone and then being able to ask that next question in a way that is meaningful and not just something I read out of a book. I'm forever grateful for those books and for all of the training I've received as it's given me the questions and an understanding of the process and the various directions to go in a solution focused conversation, and now I feel free to listen and ask the next question instead of feeling like I need to 'get through' a whole list of questions.

Over time, I kept studying and taking in as much as I possibly could. This led me to become a practice supervisor within my agency, but I wanted to do more. I wanted to use this in other places and spread SF as far as I could. So while still working for the family preservation service, I developed a private practice while also doing more teaching and training. I still keep my hand in the clinical work, with two to three days a week in the difficult area of family preservation.

I also spent a number of years working with the Young Women's Trust, an organization for women ages 16 to 30 in the United Kingdom, supporting economic equality. Most of the young women are unemployed and working for low pay, and the organization provides coaching as well as job application services. I was part of a group that provides telephone coaching and used my solution focused skills to help phone clients discover the steps they wanted to take in their lives. One of the most common dilemmas was around making the 'right' decision. My solution focused training helps me stay away from simple advice giving or trying to answer that impossible question of, 'what should I do?' For example, when a client asked me to tell her if she should risk leaving her present dead-end job or stay for stability's sake and see if things improved, I answered by asking "Let's say you've picked the one that's right for you, how will you be living once you've made your decision?" This question helped the client think more about how she wanted to be living day to day and what her quality of life would be like. From there, she knew which option would then enable her to live in that way.

I'm always interested in learning more and listening to others and how they use the solution focused approach, which is one of the massive benefits of the SFU. While being part of a dedicated solution focused service is amazing, I know that I'm incredibly lucky to have people around me to bounce ideas off, ask questions, practice with, etc. And at the same time, it's always nice to see and hear other people work as there is always something to learn – no matter how much training I've had.

I love applying my solution focused orientation across a variety of settings – whether it's with families, supervision, coaching, training, working with groups; the commonalities are being human, staying in the moment, listening to people, having a profound respect for clients and their strengths, and holding on to the idea that change is possible – that things can be better. I continue to believe in infinite possibilities just as I did flying across the ocean all those years ago.

Questions for the Reader:

1.   How does Greg open up the idea of "infinite possibilities" with his clients?

2.   How is he able to introduce change in the context of a possibly brief phone call, through his work with the Young Women's Trust?

SOLUTION FOCUSED THERAPY IN PRIVATE PRACTICE

Rachelle Bloksberg *(tele-therapy)*
Donna Harper-Hinton *(faith based private practice)*

Rachelle Bloksberg

I work three days a week in private practice. My practice is entirely online, using technology to work with clients. Online therapy fits with my independent perspective. I and my husband, an attorney, are entrepreneurs and flourish in a small rural town in Northern California.

When I decided I wanted to go back to school and become a marriage and family therapist to augment my neurofeedback practice, my greatest fear was I would have to close off a part of myself to practice at an uncomfortable professional distance. I liked connecting with my clients and didn't want to stop. I also thought I would have to follow a strict protocol that was much the same for every client. I was so relieved when I found Solution Focused Brief Therapy so early on! I never had to unlearn and relearn so I could be the therapist I wanted to be. I started taking Elliott's courses while I started my master's program. Thanks to Elliott's training, I didn't have to give up being myself at work. I didn't have to follow the same cookie-cutter process with each and every client. There is such freedom in asking questions built with the client's language. I don't plan ahead for what each session will cover. I get to use my "go with the moment" mentality. I see sessions as improvisational conversations that build on what my client says. I get to treat each client like the valuable individual they are. I get to be surprised and go with what the client brings to each session. It's such an honor to watch my clients change how they want to change.

I closed her neurofeedback practice and started her private psychotherapy practice during COVID-19. I had already done tele-therapy with veterans and their families for three years before it became the norm during COVID-19.

I have loved online therapy from the very start. COVID gave me the opportunity to close my physical office and go entirely online. Now, all my clients are used to tele-therapy and have realized its many benefits. They are just as comfortable being themselves online as they were in office. I have never had a client be anxious about using a tele-therapy platform or being in front of a camera. It hasn't even come up as a topic for discussion. My clients follow my lead of being natural and comfortable meeting them online.

I find that tele-therapy expands my practice. I can see clients throughout the state of California. My rural location with little diversity doesn't limit my client base. I find my practice has had so much more diversity online. I have worked with active-duty military, veterans, the LGBTQ+ community, and people of color. I consider it an honor to be able to support so many people from a wide range of backgrounds.

When a prospective client calls, I only answer what they ask. I don't mention that her practice is solution focused unless they ask. I pays attention to their needs. The call is about them, not the therapist. I keep answering the questions clients ask. I want them to feel respected and heard. I never push or hard sell to get someone to schedule. That's not how I want to start our therapeutic relationship. We are both screening at the same time for compatibility. It is important to me to only have clients who fit my experience and energy level.

Work-life Balance with Tele-therapy

I find it essential to set clear boundaries between work and home life. Work email, text, and phone calls stop when my workday ends. After hours, I rarely answer an email, call, or text from a prospective client. I don't want to set the precedent of being available 24/7.

Benefits of Tele-therapy

Self-care

Tele-therapy allows me to take the best care of myself. I have several chronic illnesses. Working from home in my recliner reduces my pain level. My feet are up to help with my circulation. I can turn on and off my heating pad as needed. My clients don't need to know how I'm caring for myself unless I want to share with them—all they can see are my head and shoulders.

Finances

In addition to physical comfort, working online reduces my financial outlay. Since I don't need an office, I spend less to run my business. (I also doesn't drive to work, so there is no gasoline cost or wear and tear on a car.) Lower overhead reduces the number of clients I need to see to break even each month, making it easier to meet my financial needs.

Quality of Life

Less time working translates into more time for me to spend doing other things I love. It also allows me to create a client schedule with downtime to recover if I overdo it physically. Currently, I only see clients three days a week. All in all, tele-therapy increases my quality of life.

Access to clients nationwide

Tele-therapy is beneficial for clients too. It is more convenient, saves time, and offers a different level of privacy. Most of my clients live far away in other parts of California. I live in Northern California, and many live in Southern California. That's eight hours away, at least. Even clients who live in the San Francisco Bay Area are 3 hours away. There is no chance of me bumping into them at the grocery store!

Privacy for clients

My waiting room is online. Clients don't have to worry about someone they know popping in and seeing them sitting in a physical waiting room and wondering why they are seeking help. My clients like this sort of privacy.

Physical limitations

One of my specialties is chronic illness. It can be difficult for clients to find a therapist who understands chronic health issues. Tele-therapy makes it easier to find a therapist specializing in a particular issue but located somewhere else in the state. People dealing with chronic illness can also have difficulty getting to appointments. It's a lot more work than you may imagine to go on an outing. Most can't just throw on some clothes, pick up their car keys and go. Instead, it's a labor-intensive process. Some have to schedule transportation with a caregiver. Another consideration is all the time and energy required to get ready and be "presentable" before even leaving the house. Getting to and from the car on both ends of the trip can add to the exhaustion.

Arriving to therapy at a high level of exhaustion makes it difficult to participate fully. Each person has logistics that can get in the way. Being in another environment can bring up lots of issues. The chair might not support their body well. The lighting could cause migraines. Scents can cause headaches, respiratory problems, or other allergic reactions. Clients may also have issues with the room temperature. Clients can avoid these barriers with tele-therapy.

My clients can have their sessions where they feel most comfortable and join me online. They can feel safe from reactions in their controlled environment. They can be present and benefit from therapy without using a large portion of their daily energy allotment.

Comfort level

Individuals and couples also reap additional benefits from online therapy sessions. They don't have to go through the hassle and expense of getting a sitter for the kids. They don't waste time and gasoline driving to and from appointments. When clients join their online sessions, they don't bring the additional stress of logistical problems and dealing with traffic. After the session is over, clients don't have the stress of getting home while in a vulnerable state. It's more comfortable for them to be vulnerable in their environment. There is a special comfort in already being at home after a session. Nobody will see clients leave an office with teary eyes with tele-therapy. They can practice self-care right away, curl up with a cup of tea, snuggle with a loved one, or relax with their pet. They can devote their full attention to what they need at that moment.

Tele-therapy fits more easily into busy lives. Many clients like to schedule their sessions during lunch. Couples can have their session during their lunch hour from separate locations. Some clients plan sessions right after work instead of wasting time in rush hour traffic. They join the session from their private office or car in their work parking lot or a nearby park. Once the session ends, they drive home without traffic, and in much less time. It is easier to fit therapy into the lives of busy parents with the flexible option of tele-therapy.

An unexpected perk: Pets!

One unexpected perk of tele-therapy for me has been meeting my client's pets. Having their pets with them can be calming. Pets can also break up a stressful moment with kisses and purrs. Clients like to talk about their pets and how their pets support them. Knowing about their pets helps me incorporate questions into the session about their pets and how they would notice and react to changes in my client.

The downside to tele-therapy and how a solution focus helps

Besides the logistics, tele-therapy is often the same as in-person therapy for me. Connecting to my clients is the same as it was in my office. I still ask the same questions and my clients still give their unique answers. We still laugh together and cry together (Remember, there is laughing in therapy!). I can still feel their emotional energy, just like I felt my grandmother's love long-distance, through the phone lines, so many years ago. Human connection is human connection. It can take place anytime there is communication. We can connect through technology just as we do when we are together in the same location.

Surprise disconnections

However, one aspect that can get in the way is the internet connection quality. I talk to my clients about getting disconnected ahead of time. I let them know I'll do her best to remember the last thing they said. Usually, all it takes to fix a connection problem is to log off and back in again. When they reconnect, I begin with, "The last thing I heard you say was . . ." Clients rarely have a problem, just continuing as if nothing had happened. A solution focused approach helps me stay on task and not dwell on these issues.

Emergency Preparedness

Another logistical issue I take care of in my intake paperwork is collecting information in case of an emergency. If I were to call 911 from my area, it wouldn't work if my client is in another county. The intake paperwork includes a section for the address and direct phone number for the client's local police department and emergency room. I also document their current location for each session if they aren't at home. If they are in their car, I record the make, model, and license plate and the location where they are parked. If an emergency occurs, I would be able to get local help for my client quickly. Having the emergency information for their exact location is reassuring and covers me legally. Again, a focus on solutions and signs of safety also helps.

Solution-focused aspects of tele-therapy

With all the benefits for the therapist and client, I think tele-therapy is here to stay and will become even more sought after. Solution focused work helps make this more possible. Technical challenges, like a poor internet connection or weather interference, become opportunities to demonstrate resilience and look for positive exceptions. The focus on constructing meaning in language with solution focused work fits with not having a need to be in the same room, but just to listen closely.

I see tele-therapy as possibly helping prospective clients overcome the social stigma of seeking help. Many people avoid therapy for fear of judgment no matter how much they may be suffering. The added privacy of tele-therapy could encourage these people to try therapy since they won't have to contend with face-to-face interactions. Tele-therapy has the potential to open up psychotherapy as an option for those who might have concerns about being seen as a person with problems. This again is a fit with the stigma reducing strengths focused approach of SFBT.

Donna Harper-Hinton

For as long as I can remember, I have been encouraged by, and held firmly to, two passages of the Bible as light posts to guide and direct my steps on my journey of Christian faith and in my life. Jeremiah 29:11 promises: "For I know the plans I have for you" declares the Lord, "plans to prosper you and not to harm you, plans to give you hope and a future." (NIV) Proverbs 3:5-6 assures: "Trust in the Lord with all your heart and lean not on your own understanding: in all your ways acknowledge him, and he will make your paths straight" (NIV)

I also knew even as a young girl that I wanted to be a counselor, someone who helped people to have hope, peace and joy and the opportunity to live their best lives. I attended Canadian Bible College in Regina, Saskatchewan, and completed a Bachelor of Religious Education (BRE). While there I took my first counseling course focused on Christian Counseling within a church context.

I taught English as an Additional Language and was an elementary school classroom teacher for many years, mostly in international schools. In 2006, when I was teaching Grade 4 at Singapore American School (SAS) I was introduced to SFBT for the first time by Debbie Hogan, who had trained with Insoo Kim Berg and Steve de Shazer and had founded the Academy of Solution Focused Training (ASFT) in Singapore. Debbie had been invited to SAS to train the SAS Counseling team in SFBT. Given my interest in counseling and emphasis on social and emotional learning (SEL) I was invited to join the training. From the first day of training with Debbie, I knew that this was the approach to counseling that resonated with my Christian and personal beliefs and how I wanted to work with people. From 2006 - 2008, while still a classroom teacher, I was able to take several modules of SFBT through ASFT from Debbie Hogan as well as from other SF experts like Therese Steiner and Linda Metcalf, that ASFT brought to Singapore.

Even as a teacher I found I was able to implement many of the things I was learning about SF in my classroom working with my students and with my colleagues and parent community. In August, I met with each of my students about their best hopes for the year, what was important to them and what they were proud of themselves for. Though it was not the expectation or common practice in my school, I invited each of my student's parents to meet with me personally during the first couple of weeks of the school year to have their own 'Best Hopes Conferences' and to hear from parents about their hopes and dreams for their child, the strengths and resources their children had, and the environment that best supported their child's learning. These meetings also established me as a partner with both my students and their parents in my student's learning, while setting my students up to give them the autonomy to make some of their own choices and take personal responsibility for their success.

SF also gave me a refined lens for how I listened to and used my student's language to help them move towards their hopes and goals, whether I was meeting with them for a reading or writing conference, supporting them in math, science or social studies, having regular check-ins and casual conversations or in a formal goal setting conference. Although I was required to give a certain amount of homework each week, I was able to empower my students to craft their own personal and flexible homework planners that included the required math and reading but gave them the room to consider their own interests, hopes, goals and schedules. As a result, my students felt valued and respected and that they had a measure of control, autonomy and voice in their classroom. They worked hard to be successful and as a bonus homework didn't become an issue for my students at home or at school.

One of the SFBT workshops that I attended at SAS was entitled WOWW, Working On What Works. At the time I had a 4th grade student, I will call Penny, who was not meeting her potential and was often sidetracked by seeking attention from her teachers and classmates for behaviors that were not supporting her learning. Other students were starting to become inpatient with Penny and she was showing some signs of frustration. I asked Penny if we could meet during a recess and chat. When we met, I asked Penny again what she was hoping for that year, what was working well for her, what she wanted more of, moments that she had enjoyed success, what she had noticed about herself in those moments, and what strengths and resources she had that had helped her. I also asked Penny about the kind of student and friend she wanted to be when the best version of herself was present in the classroom. At the end of our conversation Penny decided how she wanted to move forward, and that she wanted to share with her parents and a few of her trusted friends what she was experimenting with and ask them to start noticing when that best version of herself showed up. It did not take long until the rest of the students in the class also noticed when this version of Penny was present, and she started experiencing greater success in her learning and in her interactions with others.

While still teaching 4th grade full time at SAS, I started my Master of Education in Counseling from SUNY Buffalo, as part of an international cohort in Singapore that included students from North America and around Southeast Asia. After I completed my Masters and practicum hours at SAS, I was eventually hired as an Elementary Counselor in the Primary Division. While Social and Emotional Learning (SEL) and Psychoeducation are both the responsibility of a school counselor, I was also able to incorporate SFBT in many aspects of my work with students, educators, support staff and parents.

My family then moved to Moscow where I was a counselor and transition team leader at the Anglo American School (AAS). While there, I had the opportunity to help build an Elementary Counseling program and to continue to learn from a few of the experts of SF. The focus of one of the Central and Eastern Europe Regional Counseling Job-Alike Conferences that I attended in Belgrade, Serbia with my AAS counseling team was focused on using SFBT as a school counselor. Evan George from BRIEF and his wife Denise Yusuf were the trainers presenting. I used my professional development funds to virtually attend Linda Metcalf's School Counseling Conference in the fall 2020 where Elliott Connie, Anne Rambo and Ben Furman were the keynote presenters. These learning opportunities for myself and fellow school counselors not only further cemented my foundation in SF but continued to move the conversation forward about the value of SF with both the counseling team at my school, and within my region and professional network which included the International School Counseling Association.

That winter and spring as political tensions in the region escalated, and amid the challenges and forced family separations of COVID, our future in Moscow began to look murky. During this time, I remembered being inspired as I had listened to Elliott Connie present and in Googling him, I found the SFU and some of Elliott's free training. I decided to join the Diamond 1, virtual training with him and Adam Froerer that spring. It was a time of great uncertainty as I contemplated the future, what my career would look like moving forward, and thought about unexpectedly repatriating to Canada after nearly 25 years as an Expat and Third Culture Adult. The training and practice opportunities were exactly what I was looking for. Through them I was introduced to not only Elliott and Adam, but Anna Francis and Cecil Walker, as well as the amazing SFU professional community. I joined the SFU and have never looked back. Through the SFU I have met so many wonderful people I now consider not only professional colleagues but dear friends.

After my husband and I made the difficult decision to leave Moscow and international life and to repatriate to Canada so we could be near our young adult daughters and our families, I went all in with the SFU. I have completed all three levels of both the Diamond, and of Hope Building Couples Counseling, the SFU Coaching Cohort and all the courses available through the SFU. I also reconnected with Debbie Hogan and finally completed the training I had started with ASFT as well as my supervision hours with Debbie, to become a Certified Solution Focused Therapist in Canada through the CCPC Global and to become a Canadian Certified Counselor. I also joined Debbie and ASFT for their level one virtual Coaching training and attend and participate in their monthly coaching circles.

When I asked one client, a young woman I will call Jessie, about the resources she had in her life to help her experience her desired outcome of having more confidence and being her authentic self, Jessie immediately responded that her faith in God, reading the Bible, and the prayer and encouragement of other Christians had all been extremely helpful to her and had given her great peace even in difficult days. At that point I was able to ask Jessie legacy questions about where and how her faith had developed, and who and what had been important to her in growing her faith. I asked her how she had managed to continue to grow her faith, even on difficult days. I asked Jessie when her faith was present for her, in just the right way, for her to experience more confidence and more of her authentic self, how she would notice. I also asked Jessie about what the significant people in her life would notice when she was more confident and more of her authentic self. These and the other questions that followed allowed Jessie to build a rich description of the presence of her desired outcome and to experience herself as living in the confidence and authenticity she desired.

For me, the premises of SF align with my faith. My hope in God is at the heart of how I view each client through a lens of love and support me in confidently seeing each client as capable of the transformation they want as they move towards their desired outcome. My faith increases my confidence as a clinician as I rely on God, to work in and through me to be of service, and to stay attuned to each client and their language, and to ask the next helpful question.

Questions for the Reader:

1.   Rachelle and Donna both have an area of specialty in their practices, which may or may not be yours. How could SFBT be a fit with your unique practice?

2.   What do you see as your niche in private practice?

SOLUTION FOCUSED THERAPY IN SCHOOLS

Chris McMullan

Anne Rambo

Chris McMullan

My name is Chris and I have come to realize over the years of my living and working that I thrive in roles that allow for being a helper, caring for the vulnerable and engaging with others to find their hope. I have a lot of experience catering to developing autonomy in others from being a children's Christian youth camp director, to a youth rugby coach then as an elementary school teacher. While these roles have been life giving, I also thought I could be offering more. I decided to go back to school to do my masters in social work so that I could support littles (children) in their mental health.

Like many of the writers in this book I was first introduced to Solution Focused Brief Therapy (SFBT) in graduate school. It was taught in a stoic and theoretical way and even though it was lifeless in class, to me this was the one modality that seemed to move with the resonant frequency of my soul. Back then, one of the aspects that I saw as influential in drawing me to this type of therapy was the lack of talking about, and listening to others problems. Instead, in SFBT, I find joy in the focus of finding difference oriented descriptions and seeing the clients grow in hope in front of my eyes.

I ended up linking most of my papers in school to this modality and reading lots of research on the topic. As my understanding of this type of therapy grew I noticed a continued spur and excitement by thinking about how I could help others with this tool. I also realized how this method of therapy seemed to link with the natural way I interact with others; I understood the logic behind the therapeutic style because it is innate within me.

THE FOUR AMIGOS

Over the last several years, I have been blessed to be trained by Elliott, Adam, Cecil and Anna through levels 1-3 of the Diamond model. As the old adage goes; 'people won't always remember the words you say but they will remember how you made them feel', and thinking back, I don't remember all of the words that these four have said in these trainings but by the end of each one of these trainings my hope continues to burn with a fervent passion. It's in this hope filled existence that I say things like, "I know I'm good at this", "I know my heart is in the work to provide hope for others", "I'm capable".

The Diamond model was a godsend for me. In school I had been regularly asking the question "But how do I do therapy?" or "What's the format I'm supposed to follow so that I know I'm actually helping clients?". Here in the Diamond model, I received that framework and much of the worrying or uncertainty of the process was mitigated. This allows me to solely be present with clients and ask change oriented questions knowing that the littles offer hope filled responses. I am now free to find ways to find how my personality aligns with the Diamond model to allow me to be my genuine self while knowing that I am being clinically effective.

A CHANGED LIFE

It's probably pretty clear by now that this modality of therapy has, and will continue to be all encompassing for me. I have noticed that the more I have involved myself in this way of doing therapy that it has had numerous positive impacts. It has even led to several public speaking events, guest lecturing on SFBT at my alma mater and being featured in the George Fox Journal for the work I am doing in schools with children (web link at the end of the chapter). In addition to this I was awarded the Kathryn Upchurch award during the SFU annual conference in recognition of my dedication and outstanding enthusiasm of being new to SFBT.

While these outward experiences of recognition have been wonderful, the most notable change has been internal. I have noticed an affectual change within me as I have spent more time involving myself with SFBT. Everyday I hear horrible stories of hurt, abuse, malice and sadness in the referrals I receive; but when I sit in that therapy room with the little one sitting in front of me and ask questions like "what lets you know that you won't always feel this way?" and they say "I'm strong", both our hopes rise. It is with this rising hope I find I see hope in the mundane of life. I notice I live a life well lived mentally, spiritually, emotionally and physically since developing the habit of noticing hope show up in spite of the hard realities of life taking place.

A LIFE CHANGER

I grew up in Ireland so I had never experienced or heard of Mr Rogers until I moved to the United States. After reading some of the books written about and by him, I realized that this was a guy he wanted to be like in life. Fred Rogers saw the awe in people and children especially in an unforced and genuine way and I have a quote in my office from Fred that still holds the same weight of significance from the first day I read it, it says;

> *"Sometimes, all it takes is one kind word to nourish another person. Think of the ripple effect that can be created. One kind, empathetic word has a wonderful way of turning into many."*

The joyful thing about SFBT is the questions clinicians ask offer ways for clients to speak kind words about themselves and end up nourishing them with their own words. It's a sacred space to sit in those moments of self affirmation and see hope rising within. I can now name numerous occasions with clients in which I saw hope arising from circumstances that were traumatic and times when kids just didn't want to talk yet ended up finding safety in their voice. Two stand out cases illustrate this growth and change.

In one case the community that I work in suffered a shooting that ended in death at the local grocery store. I was referred to connect with a 4th grader who had witnessed this murder as she was in the same line as the victim waiting to check out with her mom. I picked up Sarah(name changed) from class and took her to the therapy room. Sarah and I started by having a snack together and then playing a short game of Uno. After some time I wondered with her "If there was something we could talk about today that would give you the most hope, what would that thing be?" Through a series of difference and meaning making questions she ended up saying "I want to be able to go to the store with my mom again without being scared". Sarah and I had a conversation about her desired hopes and when the time felt right and trust had been built I asked "What lets you know that you won't always be afraid to go to the store?". Sarah paused for a moment and said, "When I moved from Mexico to Oregon I was really scared because I didn't know English and I had no friends here, but now I'm not scared of that anymore so, I might not always be afraid to go to the store again".

The second case which resonates was when I was asked to work with a 2nd grader named Jose(name changed). Jose was a foster child who did not communicate with adults and was lacking in his academics for multiple reasons. For the first session, there were no responses from Jose even when I asked questions to engage. The only reply came at the end of the session when I asked Jose if he would like to get together next week and spend some time, to which Jose nodded affirmatively. The next week came and Jose and I strolled to the therapy room. While walking to the room I noticed that Jose had light-up Buzz Lightyear shoes on and I said to Jose, "Those shoes look really fun!". As the two walked into the therapy room and Chris closed the door he heard a voice behind him say, "Buzz Lightyear is my favorite toy". I and Jose had a conversation about Buzz and all the things his toy could do including popping out wings and a button to make the toy talk as well as light up a laser. Jose even went into detail about the marks and scratches on this toy but still recognized its value to him. After some conversation, I shifted the conversation to an SFBT formulated line of questioning at which point, Jose became quiet again. I wondered what had changed and decided to pivot questioning to involve Buzz. I said to Jose, who was playing with fidgets, "let's play an imagination game". I then asked Jose to imagine that his Buzz toy was sitting in the chair that I was sitting in. I adjusted my posture and voice to mimic the toy and even asked where the button was on the toy to pop out the wings at which point Jose pushed an imaginary button and my arms flew up pretending to be wings. Jose was smiling and seemingly relishing the imagination. I then used some of the language of Buzz that Jose had talked to me about to frame a best hopes question. I said "What do you want to talk about today that would give you hope to infinity and beyond?". Through the whole session Jose engaged and talked while I threw my voice to be like Buzz Lightyear in the movies. Jose was talking to an adult in a way that was important to him.

In both these cases, the kids' hopes rose by asking them questions that had meaning to each of them. Harkening back to the quote by Fred Rogers, if one were to replace 'empathetic word' with 'hopeful question', this quote is true of SFBT.

If I have learned anything from working with children either in the United States or back home in Ireland, the same singular rule rings true. Children value intentional attention from an adult that they know cares about them and I have found no better way to express his belief in, and care for a child than in the way he asks them questions that thrusts their hope forward.

https://www.georgefox.edu/journalonline/summer23/feature/
hero-for-superheroes.html

Anne Rambo

I am a consultant to the Broward county school district, the sixth largest school district in the United States, and one which serves 271,500 students from 204 different countries, speaking 191 different languages (www.browardschools.com). I am also chair of the American Association for Marital and Family Therapy's Family Therapists in Schools Interest Network, and faculty at Nova Southeastern University's couple and family therapy program. These three roles come together when I take couple and family therapy interns out to the public schools with me to work in the district's innovative Alternative to External Suspension Intensive (AESI) program.

AESI builds on a district wide program started in 2013. At the time, the Broward school district was being sued by the national NAACP and the Florida branch of NAACP, along with individual parents, for its high rate of schoolhouse arrests, and disproportionate rate of suspensions for students of color. This is a national problem, well documented for its damaging effect on young people of color, young men in particular (Mallett, 2016). Then superintendent of schools Robert Runcie put together a coalition of law enforcement, community advocates, and schools, to create an alternative to suspension and arrest. This diversion program was known as the PROMISE program, now renamed AESI. Unusually, from the beginning, the NSU couple and family therapy program was involved as a resource. Master's interns from the program are an integral part of the program, seeing every student suspended through the program, under my supervision. Since 2013, the program has reduced schoolhouse arrests by 63% (www.browardintervention.org), reduced overall suspensions by 25% (www.browardintervention.org), and reduced recidivism (defined as the student being suspended twice in the same school year) from 38% to 9% at the high school level (Mendel, 2018).

Given that the program exists within and because of a national context of injustice, the MS interns in the program practice what we consider to be a social justice informed version of Solution-Focused Brief Therapy. I have been greatly influenced by Elliott Connie's work on social justice and SFBT (https://elliottconnie.com/social-justice/). At the AESI Program, interns take on the role of solution focused advocates in order to include the wider societal context and honor their client's voices. They do this by connecting students and their families to school district resources and information; assisting them in finding allies while learning how to advocate for themselves; helping parents navigate the larger system of the school district; and building relationships between the students, their families, and school officials.

Working with social justice issues, and with a marginalized community of young people, means that conflict cannot at times be avoided. For the NSU team working with what was then known as the PROMISE program, that time of conflict came after the Parkland school shooting. On Valentine's Day 2018, a 19-year-old who had been expelled from the school district entered Stoneman Douglas High School with an assault rifle and opened fire. As the shooting unfolded one of the NSU MS faculty was teaching a couple therapy class for master's students;

suddenly a master's student screamed out loud. The student had received a text from her younger brother, telling her that he was hiding in a classroom and expected to be shot any minute. He was texting to say he loved her and to say goodbye. Students and faculty alike rushed to news media to follow the unfolding events. This student's brother survived unhurt, though traumatized; 17 at Stoneman Douglas were killed, however, and 16 injured. The experience profoundly affected the community including our student community (Rambo et al, 2019, p.14).

Naturally students and faculty rushed to provide services to those affected. To their surprise, however, their work in the schools quickly became a target. The National Rifle Association clashed with the student supervisors of the massacre who formed the March for Our Lives organization and advocated fiercely for gun control (as they continue to do). Specifically, the NRA opposed the March for Our Lives group's attempts to get a red flag gun law passed in Florida (such a law allows law enforcement to confiscate in advance the weapons of those repeatedly involved in domestic violence and/or making credible threats to shoot others). Seeking for other, not gun related, causes, the NRA sent employees to the area to focus attention on the PROMISE program, as representing an ethic of being soft on student crime (https://www.huffpost.com/highline/article/parkland/).

For me, it was a time of trial. I was advised by some university administrators to distance myself from the PROMISE program, which I refused to do. While I was not personally threatened, I know firsthand that district employees who were supporters of the PROMISE program received credible death threats. At one point, the local newspaper ran a headline that the PROMISE program was to be closed. I and my interns, the school district employees, and the students themselves continued as usual, waiting to hear a more official verdict. Eventually, the newspaper was forced to print a retraction. It was definitively proved the Parkland shooter had never attended PROMISE (https://www.huffpost.com/highline/article/parkland/). Then governor Rick Scott's Marjorie Stoneman Douglas High School Public Safety Commission recommended the continuation and even the expansion of the PROMISE program (https://www.browardschools.com/cms/lib/FL01803656/Centricity/Domain/13726/PROMISE%20Program%20Update%20June%202019.pdf). And in addition, Florida passed a red flag gun law against the NRA's recommendations and with bipartisan support (https://www.cnn.com/2022/06/01/politics/florida-red-flag-law/index.html). This law has resulted in thousands of weapons confiscated before a violent crime was committed.

And so, with respect to the PROMISE program, everything returned to "normal". However, the program was subsequently renamed. The lesson for me and my interns was that programs which truly change lives must be explained and defended; true social change can never be taken for granted. An activist role is needed.

What is it that we do which is so "different" that it stirs up controversy? This case example may provide a glimpse.

Case Example

As the MS interns need experience, usually I confine my role to live supervision (easy to do as the interns and suspended students meet in the large alternative school cafeteria, in groups of two (one student and one intern each), and I can walk around to each group and make comments).   But on days when the number of students suspended is high, or the situations more complicated, sometimes I take a turn seeing student clients myself. On a recent weekday, I found there was a student "left over" after all the other suspended students that day had been assigned to interns. Checking to see that all the interns were doing well, I returned to this student and let him know he could talk with me, if he preferred that to waiting.

I asked the student (let's call him Frank, not his real name) about his hopes for after he graduated from high school. Frank wasn't sure what he wanted to do, but he was clear he wanted to graduate from high school, and that he did not want to end up incarcerated like his father. He mentioned how carefully his mother watched over him, and how worried she was about his suspension for a schoolboy prank gone wrong. I congratulated him on having such a caring, concerned mother, and he agreed. He worried aloud that he wasn't very academic, and that while he wanted to do right and stay out of trouble, he got bored easily. He and I chatted about what a strength, even a super-power, getting bored easily and therefore being willing to live on the edge can be. I mentioned firefighters and being an emergency medical technician, just as examples of heroes among us who live on the edge. Frank perked up and asked if I knew of any ways a person could learn about such things. It just so happened I had a flyer for a local program which trains young people to become fire fighters and EMTs while still in high school. (We have a myriad of flyers for all sorts of options.) Frank's face lit up, and he carefully folded the flyer into thirds and put it in his back pocket, so he would be sure not to lose it. The rest of the time passed pleasantly with Frank and I talking about his bright future, including his dreams of helping his mother out financially and one day being a present father to his children. After about 45 minutes, I noticed it was now time for this student's age group to go outside for recess. I suggested to him that they could talk more tomorrow if he liked, but that he was now free to go outside and play. His face lit up, but then fell. He whispered "I wish I could but I can't – they won't let me – they told me I had to see a counselor or I would fail the program. I think I have to see a counselor." "That was me" I explained. He looked bewildered. I explained again "That was me. I was the counselor. You did talk to me." I wish I had a photo of his astonished face! "Really?" he said, "You were the counselor? But you just talked to me like I was a person!" A few days later I saw this student in the hall. He called her over to say he had called the EMT training program and was signed up.

This is ultimately the most "revolutionary" thing about SFBT – that we are human with our clients.

References:

1.	Mallett, C.A.	(2016) "The School-to-Prison Pipeline: A Critical Review of the Punitive Paradigm Shift" *Child Adolesc Soc Work J 33,* 15–24 https://doi.org/10.1007/s10560-015-0397-1

2.	Rambo, A., Erolin, K., Beliard, C., & Almonte, F. (2019). "Through the Storm: How a Master's Degree Program in Marriage and Family Therapy came to new understandings after surviving both a natural and a human disaster within six months" In L. Charles and G. Samarasinghe (Eds.) *Global Humanitarian Mental Health* pp.

Questions for the Reader:

1.	Both Chris and Anne stress being human with their child clients. How is this a fit with solution focused therapy?

2.	What would it mean to have more solution focused therapists in the school system?

SOLUTION FOCUSED WORK WITH MARGINALIZED POPULATIONS

Rebekka Ouer

Rebekka Ouer

I have worked in private practice since 2011, specializing in the LGBT community in an area that is locally known as "the gayborhood" in Dallas, Texas.

I was first introduced to SFBT when I saw Insoo Kim Berg speak at a mental health conference in San Antonio in the summer of 2003. I felt an instant connection to the ideas and beliefs that Insoo shared, specifically the tenet that you can simply trust and believe in your clients as amazing and capable humans, without judgment or focusing on problematic diagnoses. Since then, I have studied under Dr. Peter Lehman, and subsequently worked with and studied under Elliott Connie. I wrote a book about my work at the intersection of SFBT and the LGBT community, titled; *SFBT with the LGBT Community; Creating futures through Hope and Resilience*. Working at that intersection in the conservative and increasingly-queerphobic state of Texas, I have learned a great deal about the impact this work can have on marginalized communities.

There is always an unequal power dynamic in a therapy room. Therapists have the power to diagnose, critique, advise, report, or to make judgements about their clients. And the client is in the vulnerable place of not knowing whether their therapist will respect that power and be safe or abuse it and prove themselves unsafe.

Unfortunately, it is all too common for clients within marginalized communities to experience abuse of that power in what should be one of the safest relationships they can have, the relationship with their therapist. SFBT, however, does a fantastic job of correcting for that power dynamic by allowing the client, with the very first question asked to define where the conversation is going. And, even when there seems to be an invitation into the problem story, as seen in the transcript below, (i.e., What do you think is important for me to know about what's going on?), there is respect for the client's hopes and deferment to what the client thinks the therapist should know in order to be able to ask the next helpful question.

As a cisgender therapist, I work hard to remain cognizant of my power and privilege in conversations with my transgender clients, and to maintain a purely safe space throughout that relationship. SFBT offers an evidence-based therapeutic avenue in which to fully trust clients to be their own experts and to move forward through their lens in a way that makes sense for them and their, unique-to-them, real-world experiences. For me, that is the most beautiful thing about being an SF purist and how it fits communities that have experienced oppression, especially where the therapist is not a part of the same marginalized community.

One of the things I write and teach about when I'm conducting trainings on the intersection of SFBT and the LGBT community highlights this fit perfectly. I point out the LGBT community only asks for one simple thing; their cry to the world around them is "Let us define ourselves, (our bodies, our identities, our love), for ourselves and respect us equally in those identities." Solution focused brief therapy was founded on the principle that our clients are the experts in their lives, which includes allowing them to define themselves for themselves in all of those ways, giving them that agency throughout the therapeutic relationship. There simply is no better avenue for empowering our LGBT clients in-session than using solution focused brief therapy. With marginalized clients of all stripes, SFBT offers equity and safety in the therapeutic conversation.

A case example follows, which highlights a specific SFBT technique I find useful, the third person perspective. (Names and details have been changed to protect confidentiality, and I got permission from "Nick" to provide this case example from their last session.)

Case Example:

I first met Nick in the spring of 2015 when, at the age of 16, his parents brought him in just a few days after he tearfully came out to them as transgender. His family was incredibly supportive, and with the help of a local clinic that specializes in working with transgender youth, he began to medically transition about a year later. Nick is now almost 24 and has been thriving since his transition began. As a young adult he still stops in for a therapy session from time to time as challenges pop up in his life. In the fall of 2021, Nick was navigating a particularly troubling issue, and so he came in for some help. Our conversation follows.

Rebekka (R): Great to see you, Nick, what are your hopes for our session today?

Nick (N): I'm in a difficult situation that I think I need some help with.

R: Okay, what do you think is important for me to know about what's going on?

N: You know I've been with my girlfriend, Katie, for several years now. It's going really well, I plan to propose soon, and we both feel as though we are in a really great place and are excited for our future. Katie's family, her mom specifically, has come a really long way in supporting us. Before we started dating, her mom had a history of being pretty queer-phobic in general. Katie and I knew each other and dated, before I transitioned back in high school, and her mom was not happy that Katie was in a relationship with me. So much so that it was a big factor when we ultimately broke up back then. But we found our way back to each other after I transitioned, and since then her mom and I have really connected. She loves me as a son now, and we've really come a long way.

R: Wow, that's a lot of growth from her.

N: Yeah, she's really worked hard to overcome her prejudices and our relationship has been a big factor in that. But that's sort of being challenged right now with this current situation.

R: Ahh, I see. Okay, go on.

N: So, Katie has a little sister, Kendall, who got a new job a couple of years ago in a small, very conservative town. Kendall has known me since she was little, back when I was in high school and dating Katie the first time. We used to be pretty close and her and Katie were VERY close, but when Kendall moved away for this job opportunity, she pretty much disconnected from everyone here. She stopped talking to Katie, to her mom, to her friends out here, she isolated with a new boyfriend she met out there and cut everyone off. It really hurt Katie and her mom that she disconnected from them that way, and they didn't understand why she was doing it. But then they learned more about the boyfriend she was with, and they felt like he might have been a factor in her decision to disconnect. He is a conservative, extreme right-wing guy from a small Texas town. When we got to know more about him, we saw posts on his social media that were very telling. He posted things that were racist, homophobic, and violently transphobic.

R: Oh my gosh….

N: Yeah, he's a young kid, maybe 19 or 20, I don't think he's actually dangerous, but he got wrapped into all of the right wing ideological politics on social media, which you know, have gotten pretty extreme these last few years.

R: Okay, I'm starting to understand a bit about your dilemma.

N: So, recently Kendall and this guy got engaged, and Kendall reached back out to the family wanting to reconnect. And of course, her mom and sister are overjoyed at the possibility of having her back in their life, they love her so much and have missed her terribly these last two years.

R: I'm sure.

N: And of course, I understand this, and honestly, I've missed her too, I've always known her to be a really good person.

R: Yeah, and still, what a scary situation this must be for you.

N: Yes…exactly. She knows I'm trans, and she has always been affirming. I just don't know if this guy, John is his name, I just don't know if John knows anything about me.

R: Ok…so how might this conversation be helpful for you, in this tough situation?

N: So, I've tried to talk to her mom a little, but she doesn't take me seriously when I say things to let her know I'm concerned about this guy. She just responds with "Oh, Nick, we won't let him hurt you." and dismisses my worries. And I don't want to push because she is so so happy to have her daughter back in the picture, I don't want to do anything to take that excitement away from her. I also don't want it to seem like I'm jealous of this guy as another future in-law, you know, like I'm worried he'll take my place or something. This isn't about that at all for me. And I'm not worried for my physical safety, it's not that either…if he doesn't know I'm trans, he'll never figure it out, I read as cis, and if he does know, I know they WOULD have my back, and not let him do anything to hurt me, he's just a young and inexperienced kid coming from his conservative bubble, I get that. I just want Katie's family to understand my discomfort and I want to know that I won't be the target of any sort of transphobia in small or big ways, either in-person or behind my back, and that if there is any transphobic rhetoric, directed at me or not, even micro-aggressions, that they will be ready with affirming push back to it. I'm just really really anxious about this and don't know how to have this conversation without taking away from their very real and understandable excitement about their daughter and sister coming back into the fold after two long years, and while making it clear that this isn't about some jealous competition between future son-in-laws.

R: Can you tell me a little about conversations you and Katie have had around this?

N: Yeah, so that's another piece of this…I'm so anxious here, I feel so guilty and confused about how to handle this, that when it gets brought up, I get defensive, and we end up fighting, so we haven't gotten very far at all in those conversations. I know Katie has my back, I know she wants me to be safe, I just don't know how to talk about this with her or how to address it effectively with her family without being overly sensitive and taking their push back personally. I don't know if they will be able to listen to me, you know, because none of them are trans or queer, so they just can't fully understand my situation. I don't want them to shut her out or shame her for getting with this guy, I just want to know that they understand what this is like for me and that they will have my back the way I know my own family would.

R: Ok I have a question for you.

N: Ok, good.

R: Do you have any friends or family members who are also part of a marginalized community? Someone who might end up in a very similar situation as a result of that difference?

N: Actually, yeah, my best friend Mario is Hispanic, his family is from Mexico, and he's in a long-term relationship with a woman who is white.

R: Ok, Nick, so here's my question…. imagine that Mario invites you out to lunch and tells you exactly what you just told me, except it's happening with him & his partner's family. If he were to come to you for something like this, what advice might you give him?

N: I'd tell him it's his partner's responsibility to be his ally where it comes to her family, and especially with this new fiancé of her sister's.

R: Can you say more about that?

N: Yeah, I mean it seems so obvious when I look at it this way, but his girlfriend's name is A.J., and I would ask him how much he trusts her, you know, if she's safe, & how much he believes that A.J. is an ally to him and to the Hispanic community, and how willing she might be to have uncomfortable conversations with her family for the sake of protecting him. I think it's clear that he can't advocate for himself in her family with the same power she has.

R: Wow, that's some great advice.

N: I just hadn't thought of it this way, but yeah, that's helpful.

R: Ok, so, how much do you trust Katie here, how much do believe in her ability to be your ally with her beloved family, and how important is it for her to do this for you?

N: I know she can, I know she will and that she would want to. I think I just have to help her understand it the same way I understand it now.

R: And how confident are you in your ability to have that conversation in a way that is right for you?

N: That will be hard…. it's such a sensitive topic for me and I get so defensive.

R: Sure, for some very good reasons. What do you hope from yourself, then, as you're navigating this sensitive, vulnerable topic with your partner?

N: I think it's remembering what I just told you. I do trust her, I know she loves me, I know she has my back. This is hard, but it's not hard because she doesn't love me, it's hard because it's hard. You know?

R: And what difference will it make for you in that conversation, to remember and hold on to that trust in her? That knowledge that she loves you and has your back, and can/would want to do this difficult thing to ensure your safety?

N: I think I won't get as defensive. It will help me stay calm and be honest and vulnerable.

R: And when she sees her boyfriend, her future husband, being vulnerable in this difficult conversation, how is she likely to react?

N: That's when she is her softest with me. She is really protective of me, and I think she'll want to be strong and do whatever is needed to help me be safe. I don't know why I didn't think of it this way before, it seems so simple.

Reflections

In this case example, Nick came in seeking help navigating a tough dilemma in his life in which he was suddenly feeling unsafe in his partner's family. A family he had previously felt very safe with. Once I understood where Nick wanted to go, I asked a question that helped him come to his own brilliant answer by helping him step outside of his own dilemma and see it from a third party's perspective, but not just any third party – I purposefully asked about someone Nick already knows and cares about. Giving this same dilemma to his beloved friend then allowed Nick to immediately think about the situation from outside of his own perspective, and as a result he was able to give his friend, and thus himself, some incredibly wise advice.

I trusted him to do just that with my question, putting him directly into that third party point of view. With this line of questioning the therapist allows the client to remain their own expert, even when they come in seemingly seeking direct advice about a very specific problem.

Seeing his dilemma from a bit outside of himself helped Nick to create a solution very quickly: a solution that fit directly with his core values as a person not only as a marginalized member of society, but also an empathic & educated ally to others. Stepping outside of his own marginalization here, to view his friend Mario's potential dilemma as a man of color in relationship with a white woman, allowed Nick to see that the person who often has the most power to make an impactful difference in a situation like his, is a close ally. For him, thinking through that outside example clarified immediately that his loving and trusted partner had an opportunity here, using her cisgender privilege, to communicate and advocate for him much more powerfully with her family than Nick would ever be able to.

This case example highlights a unique opportunity present between therapists and members of marginalized communities to empower those clients using a solution focused approach. When the client comes to the therapist with a problem that needs solving, the therapist has so many options for how to go about helping them. Following solution focused tenets creates some powerful opportunities to lead from behind, as Insoo often reminded us in her teachings and writings. And one of the most powerful paths of therapeutic questioning that SFBT has honed brilliantly, is this third person perspective.

Questions for the Reader:

1.	How do you see Rebekka's solution focused approach as a fit with social justice issues?

2.	How is her approach a fit with honoring social justice issues?

SOLUTION FOCUSED STORY TELLING

Edward Eisemann

Edward R. Eisemann was for many years the clinical director of Unitas, an innovative outreach program to African-American and Puerto Rican youth in the South Bronx. Edward, or "Doc" as everyone called him, was a founding member of the Solution Focused University. He was asked to contribute a chapter on his work with Unitas, but instead he sent wonderful stories – stories that reflect his skill as a solution focused storyteller. Edward R. Eisemann died on June 26, 2023, at the age of 91. The stories that follow are in his own words.

Story One:

An old, wise, owl observed a little girl holding a puppy close to her heart. It wondered what this puppy felt and asked, "What are your best hopes as you are held so lovingly?" The puppy said, "My hope is to be this way forever." "And," the owl continued, "what difference would that make for you as you grow up?" Puppy said, "I know from what I feel here that I would always be safe, loved and valued all my life." Owl went on and said, "What would you be able to do with this kind of caring that you could not do without it?" There was no question in the puppy's mind. "I would be able to love everyone in the world wherever they are, even beyond the earth."

One lucky pup! And one lucky world!

Story Two:

I received a wonderful comment from a colleague sharing with me her thoughts that it seemed that I was a natural animal SFT practitioner, a practice she herself is promoting, called animal assisted therapy. With her inspiring comment to me and support, I am continuing my SFT stories on animals here, but now adding to my talk to the animal companion that I _am_ going to talk to the dog using a therapy model of conversation.

Again, in my daily treks in my forestry park I met a man with a beautiful lab dog, which dog came to me in a friendly way, wagging his tail and waiting to be ruffled. As usual, I said to his caretaker," He is so friendly, how did he learn this?" A long story followed about the dog originally being trained as a seeing eye dog by his daughter. In her training him, the dog, as a puppy, went wherever she went, side by side and was treated kindly. After a year she gave the lab dog to him. I said, "What difference did that make for you to get such a friendly dog?" He smiled and said, "The dog was not only friendly but so obedient as well from her kind training of him. Even when I put his food down, he will not eat until I say 'ok'."

Again, I asked what difference this dog made for him in his life. With heart in his voice he said, "He has brought such a joy into my life, especially now with some concerns of my own that I worry about. But I have this dog! And that's what makes the difference!

One lucky pup! One lucky man!

Story Three:

As I trekked through my wonderful forestry park today, I met a beautiful and gentle dog walking slowly with its caretaker. I went close and said, "What a beautiful dog. What are some hopes this dog has?" The caretaker said, "Just to be out here taking a slow, peaceful and enjoyable walk." I said, "What difference does that make for this dog?" She said, "He is filled with relaxation and enjoyment just being here and doing this. "I said, "What do you notice about him that tells you that he feels this way?" She says, "I can tell from the way he looks and walks that he is in these states of feeling."

I said, "What does he notice about you that lets him know you notice these things about him?" She says something like, "He knows from the way I am with him here, walking and enjoying myself." Time was up, so I could not pursue this evolving rich conversation with further inquiry about the details of "enjoyment," and "relaxation", but after further exploring the details I would like to have then said, "When he wakes up in the morning, what is the first thing he would notice about himself that would let him know 'today is going to be another wonderful day'?"

As we finished our flowing conversation, I said that I was a writer/therapist and would like to write up this conversation into a story form. She said immediately, "I knew that about you. You are an intelligent man, and you do this." I said I was having a therapeutic kind of conversation with the dog through her and would like to post this story, without names, in my Facebook network. She was pleased about this as we left each other. As we departed, I noticed a smile, exhilaration, an uplifted spirit, and a waving goodbye from her in this leaving.